COOL
Memories

COOL Memories

Jean Baudrillard

Translated by Chris Turner

VERSO

London · New York

First published as *Cool Memories: 1980–1985* by Editions Galilée, Paris 1987
This edition published by Verso 1990
Reprinted 1994, 2003
© This translation 1990 Verso

Verso
UK: 6 Meard Street, London W1F 0EG
USA: 180 Varick Street, New York, NY 10014–4606

Verso is the imprint of New Left Books

British Library Cataloguing in Publication Data
Baudrillard, Jean
    Cool memories.
    1. Western culture
    I. Title   II. Cool memories. *English*
    909.098210828

    ISBN 0-86091-283-3
    ISBN 0-86091-500-X pbk

US Library of Congress Cataloging-in-Publication Data
Baudrillard, Jean.
    [Cool memories, 1980–1985. English]
    Cool memories / Jean Baudrillard : translated by Chris Turner.
      p. cm.
    Previously published as: Cool memories, 1980–1985, 1987.
    ISBN 0-86091-283-3. — ISBN 0-86091-500-X (pbk.)
    I. Title
    PQ2662.A853483C6613   1990
    848'.91403—dc20

Typeset by Leaper & Gard Ltd, Bristol, England
Printed in Great Britain by The Bath Press, Avon

CONTENTS

OCTOBER 1980

The first day of the rest of your life

The initial stunning impact of the deserts and California is gone, and yet, to be fair, is there anything more beautiful in the world? It seems unlikely. I have to assume, then, that I have come across – *once in my life** – the most beautiful place I shall ever see. It is just as reasonable to suppose I have also met the woman whose beauty stunned me most and whose loss wounded me most. A second eventuality of the same order is unlikely – in any case the freshness, the artlessness of the event would be lost. It is just as probable that I have also written the one – or two – best books I shall ever write. They are done with. That is how things go. And it is most unlikely that a second burst of inspiration will alter this irreversible fact.

This is where the rest of life begins.

But the rest is what is given to you as something extra, and there is a charm and a particular freedom about letting just anything come along, with the grace – or ennui – of a later destiny.

*In English in original. [Tr.]

It is always possible to tell yourself that it is not tomorrow but the day after which is the first day of the rest of your life, and that it is not this face or this landscape, but the one after. That is why the thirteenth is still the first – and always the only one.*

The order of the world is always right – such is the judgement of God. For God has departed, but he has left his judgement behind, the way the Cheshire Cat left his grin.

Melancholy is just as much an affectation as *joie de vivre* – who is happy to be alive? Beings, like things, are naturally prostrate and only manage to seem happy by a superhuman effort, which has a great deal of affectation in it, but this is more in line with the involution of things.

There is a nostalgia in dialectics, in the work of Benjamin and Adorno for example. The most subtle dialectics always end in nostalgia. By contrast, and more profoundly (in Benjamin and Adorno themselves), there is a *melancholy* of the system which is incurable and invulnerable to dialectics. It is this melancholy which is gaining the upper hand today, through ironically transparent forms.

With the truth, you need to get rid of it as soon as possible and pass it on to someone else. As with illness, this is the only way to be cured of it. The person who keeps truth in his hands has lost.

*This is a reference to Nerval's sonnet 'Artémis' in *Les Chimères*. [Tr.]

4

Anyway we are condemned to social coma, political coma, historical coma. We are condemned to an anaesthetized disappearance, to a fading away under anaesthesia. If that's the case, better to feel ourselves dying, even in the convulsions of terrorism, than to disappear like ectoplasms which no one, even desensitized, will want to conjure up later to give themselves a fright.

You never know what it is that seduces you. What you are sure of is that this was meant for you. There is no other feeling that brings with it such a sense of clear self-evidence. Something has your name on it, irrevocably and at a single stroke – you have the chance to dispense with the abominable psychological labour to which we are condemned even more surely than we are condemned to social labour, and to enter total absolution.

During the making of a porn film, one of the girls – blonde with a black velvet neckband – goes through all the various acts without a change of expression. Her indifference is seductive.

In the middle of the revelries, a man whispers into the woman's ear: '*What are you doing after the orgy?*'*

It is not the figure of seduction that is mysterious, but that of the subject tormented by his own desire or his own image.

Death too becomes conspicuous by its absence.

*In English in original. [Tr.]

Marvellous, enchanting mobility, aerial alertness: cats.

All seduction is feline. It is as though appearances had begun working on their own and were unfolding effortlessly.

Felinity of appearances. All unfolding smoothly, without disruption. For felinity is simply the sovereign unfolding of the body and movement.

Better than those women who climax are those who give the impression of climaxing, but maintain a sort of distance and virginity beneath the pretence of pleasure, for they oblige us with the offer of rape.

Depth isn't what it used to be. For if the nineteenth century witnessed the long process of the destruction of appearances and their supplanting by meaning, the twentieth, subsequently, saw an equally massive process of the destruction of meaning . . . and its replacement by what? We find pleasure neither in appearances nor in meaning.

Lacan is right: language does not convey meaning. It stands in place of meaning. But the results produced are not effects of structure, but seduction effects. Not a law which regulates the play of signifiers, but a rule which ordains the play of appearances. But perhaps all this means the same thing.

When things reach that apogee where they clarify and resolve themselves, they then with equal suddenness become unintelligible and ungraspable.

There are cultures which can only picture their origins and not their ends.

Some are obsessed by both.

Two other positions are possible: only picturing one's end – our own culture; picturing neither beginning nor end – the coming culture.

Revolution – including the revolution of desire – is even less kind to those who think it has already happened than to those who oppose it. Thus it is not the Revolution which will turn me into a woman. That will come about by my espousing here and now – passionately – the position of femininity itself. Now for feminists this is unpardonable. For this position is more feminine, with all the supreme femininity it implies, than that of women will ever be.

In the general sexual confusion that reigns among us, it is almost a miracle to belong to your own sex (Émile).

Women are like historical events: they happen once in our lives as events and they are then entitled to a second existence as farce. The event of seduction, the farce of psychology. The event of passion, the farce of the work of mourning.

Fortunately, it is the same the other way round. You very probably have the good fortune to enjoy a second existence in the minds of the women you have known, as melancholy farce.

By a single nuance, a single word charged with unconscious hatred, you know it's over. And yet you have to go right on to the end, with all the vicissitudes of love and their twisting psychological paths. None of that has any other meaning than to bring you back to the first moment, when you saw in a blinding flash that the break had come.

Such is the pathos of our psychology: everything is there right at the beginning, in a single feature, a single gesture, all of whose consequences will have to be played out to the finish. But the unfolding of these will change nothing. The only use of all this is to provide the gods with a spectacle of time. And psychology is merely a discursive convulsion, when things have really occurred long before in the cursive mode of the single stroke that effects them.

Philosophy and psychology died at the same moment as 'the other', and the desire for the other, died. Only the empty sign of their concept shines out now, in a sky devoted to the mental simulacrum and the pataphysical comfort of our great cities.

Urbino Gubbio Mantua.
The beauty of these low doors opening on to successive rooms, the slipping of these perfect rectangles one inside the other. A violent eroticism produced by the geometric and hierarchical regularity of the buildings. Moving from one room to another, changing spaces is erotic. Not sexual: but belonging to that ideality of seduction in which the difference between the sexes appears like a subtle and aesthetic clue to the duality of things, an innovation, a surprise, before the Manichean violence of sex irrupts.

The real is not threatened by its double today (Clément Rosset): it is threatened by its very idiocy.*

---

*This is a reference to Rosset's 'Le Réel et son double'. [Tr.]

8

The Gift (too moral, too Christian)
Expenditure (too Romantic, too transgressive, too aesthetic)
Desire (too energetic, too repressed, too liberating)
Debt (nothing can be redeemed – too religious)
　　All the analytico-revolutionary utopias revolve around these four 'concepts' which reverberate with one another.
　　Some heresies are more paradoxical. Sovereignty (Bataille), cruelty (Artaud), the simulacrum (Klossowski). Seduction.

　　The beauty of the Aztec myth: it is by their death that the gods, one by one, give birth to light, the stars, the sky, the earth and men.

　　Just as the migrations of the Guayaki carried off the surplus population, in a state of quasi-suicidal exaltation, to the edges of the ocean where they disappeared, analysis carries off concepts to the limit point of their absolute reversibility, to their resolution in the oceanic form of a vertiginous metaphor that absorbs them.

Warm and soft and subtle: the body before lovemaking.
Fresh, soft and ductile: the flesh of seduction.
Mobile and violent and metaphysical: the form of the face.
Gentle and weary and subtle: the body after lovemaking.

What was polar and axial has become orbital and nuclear
What was historical and genetic has become tactical and a media event
What was perspectival and relational has become tactile and involutive

What was final and causal has become aleatory.
etc., etc.

Analysis is part of the immense process of the glaciation of meaning. Competition between theories is quite secondary by comparison with their joint commitment to the operation of dissection and transparency. Whatever you analyse and however you do it, you are helping to give primacy to desert forms, indifferent forms.

Fortunately, stupidity remains the sanctuary of the referent, the indestructible refuge of meaning. Unfortunately, even that fundamental stupidity has become merely a fossilized monster. He who believes in meaning will perish by meaning, or will be buried beneath the irony of appearances.

A party to which everyone brings the most stupid person they know. The person who comes up with the most stupid one wins. A risky bet, as you can never be sure with stupidity. It is unlikely an intelligent man will not say something silly in the course of the evening, nor that a stupid person will not say something clever, or simply keep silent, which will turn things around and make the person who brought them seem ridiculous. The person who brought them is no longer the person you thought they were. Intelligence speculates upon stupidity; it forgets that any quality taken to its extreme gains the upper hand over any other. As in the game of 'scissors, stone, paper', the cycles always bring the superior powers back down to an inferior position. Raised to the power of x, stupidity holds intelligence in check. It really sorts it out. Called in to serve as a mirror, it becomes seductive in its own right, and intelligence comes to seem odious.

Leukaemia, the proliferation of white blood cells at the expense of red, is universal. As is whiteness, the neutralization of the spectrum of colours in white light, the neutralization of make-up, artifice and violent seduction in the anaemic exhaustion of our white culture. The universality of that culture is that of the colour of mourning. So beautiful when it is the colour of snow or salt, lethal when it is that of blood in leukaemia or of the blank, expressionless voice in aphonia or noise in sensory deprivation – the end of racial flesh-tints, the whiteness of the operational.

If we look closely at the ambiguity of technology, we observe the constellation, the stellar motion of the secret (Heidegger).

What is hanging over us now is not hysteria or schizophrenia or even paranoia (though this latter should logically become dominant in the near future), but, in the more or less long term, melancholia. With its precursor, hypochondria, that derisory signalling of overcathected, enervated bodies and organs, rendered sad by involution. All systems, especially political ones, are virtually hypochondriacal: they manage and ingest their own dead organs.

The opposite state to passion is convalescence. We are currently in a state of sexual convalescence – everyone is still quite willing to engage in seduction, but they are weary in advance of the sexual consequences. Seduction remains the only vital intensity; sex is simply tiring, it is merely a bonus of pleasure.

She has left for Frankfurt by a different flight. The modern forms of transit which create unprecedented opportunities immediately destroy them by the same means. The media inform us; airports separate us.

Trieste – European nihilism here takes on the charm of autumn vines plunging into the sea, beneath the south wind, the karst cliffs, where oil refineries gleam on the horizon like the final solution. A few concepts too fluid to inhabit the present for very long dip and wheel on the crests of the waves, above the ironic transparency of the sea.

The hands of women are affecting, feverish, fragile. They are symbolically more manifest and more diaphanous than their sexual organs. Their hands and hair. Would the woman who offered her eyes to him cut off her hands for someone who told her they were even more seductive than her gaze?
Inanimate, translucent hands, women's hands jealous of each other.

Appearance, like freshness, is a passion. There is an obsession with truth, but a passion for appearance. That is why appearance is a ceremonial act, in a way that the act of thinking never is. However, intelligence is the seductive form of thought, just as the secret is the seductive form of truth.

The passion that attaches to the mode of production is jealousy: a God jealous of reality, jealous of appearances, jealous of meaning, jealous of interpretation, a jealous guardian of wealth and exchange. But there are also ideas jealous of their meaning, women jealous of their beauty, victims jealous of the privilege of being so, concepts jealous of each other.

Nothing will ever equal the ceremonial obstinacy of trees in their adornment, of light in its daily ritual, of wind and death in their uninterrupted cycle. The meticulous passion of silence. Ideas are merely paradoxical pathways.

Two forms of breakup: the one the result of being too far apart, the other of being too close. A break in the current, a breaking of the spell. Such closeness, day after day, for thousands and thousands of desert miles, can become unbearable as a crime. And it was indeed something like that.

When the snow falls with that supernatural slowness it has, it seems that the reasons for dying are more subtle than the reasons for living. But perhaps these latter are more numerous.

The only women loved: those whose faces come infinitely close, whose features become increasingly distinct to the touch, inciting you to a boundless caress, like a mirage engulfing all sensual emotion, in the contemplation of a thousand or more pure signs, the whole of sex encapsulated in an effect of admiration.

The only seductive theory: the one in which concepts recede to infinity, lose themselves in features ever more extreme, lending themselves to indefinite paradox, to the point of inertia where conceptual emotion is engulfed in the discovery of a thousand pure signs, and the passion for their disappearance.

We ought to find *Doctor Strangelove* reassuring: the nuclear confrontation is so unimaginable it would take a madman to unleash it. This is a sign of the degree to which the imagination fails to measure up to the possibility of nuclear war. As does reality for that matter.

Everything that can be said on the nuclear threat has already been said. Nothing has ever happened. 'Our nuclear submarines cannot all be knocked out at once and our enemy knows it, etc.' Nothing will ever happen. It is a system of general terror. But we are as if turned to stone by this potential destruction.

Overwhelmed by the fact that it never will happen. This permanent suspense is our provisional eternity.

If, in days gone by, it was sound strategy to accumulate the effects of alienation, today it is safer to stockpile the effects of indifference. To create a pole of indifference so that powerful processes of attraction or repulsion are produced all around.

To create a gulf which will swallow up inverse energies at differential speeds, on the extraordinary lines of Edgar Allan Poe's maelstrom.

Or, yet again, to become nothing but a ghostly hologram, a laser outline – so that it may then be all the easier to disappear without being noticed, leaving others prey to reality.

Dying is nothing, you have to know how to disappear.

Seeing the features of a face in closeup gives you the same dizzy feeling as a low-angle shot of a skyscraper. The vertigo of anamorphosis. The beauty of cheeks and lips smooth as a desert, a beauty equalled only by that of the skyscraper seen from below like an upturned throat.

Democracy is the menopause of Western society, the Grand Climacteric of the body social. Fascism is its middle-aged lust.

When everything turns in on itself towards a trance-like state of imaginary latency, but one still dreaming of final solutions, when all the tensions within us dissolve into a subliminal state, then it still remains for us to find the point of inertia and normalize everything by a process of destruction.

The true artificial satellite is the mass of floating currencies orbiting the earth. Money has become an artifact pure and simple, with sidereal mobility and instant convertibility, and has at last found its true home, a place more extraordinary even than the Stock Exchange: an orbit where it rises and sets like an artificial sun.

Black is the derision of White. The amazing Idi Amin who has himself carried in triumph by four British diplomats and is received by the Pope. The amazing Emperor Bokassa eating up little black babies, lavishing diamonds upon the Western dignitary. Nowhere has the concept of power been ridiculed in such an Ubuesque fashion as in Africa. The West will be hard-pressed to rid itself of this generation of simiesque and prosaic despots born of the monstrous crossing of the jungle with the shining values of ideology.

Let us remember the *Maîtres-Fous** where the lumpen-employees of the bush go home at night to the forest to mime in epileptic, frothing trances the white clerk, the white chief of Abidjan and even locomotives! All of them Bokassas, all of them Amins. Fantastic! There is no hope for this continent. All the Peace Corps will get bogged down there. The power of derision. Africa's contempt for its own 'authenticity'.

Politicians – power itself – are abject because they merely embody the profound contempt people have for their own lives. Their abjection reflects the abjection of the governed, who thereby find some way of ridding themselves of their own sense of abjection. One should be grateful to the politicians for accepting the abjectness of power, and ridding others of its burden. This inevitably kills them but they get their revenge by passing on to others the corpse of power. This ancient hereditary function has never been repudiated.

*A reference to the film by Jean Rouch. [Tr.]

It is announced that the United States of Africa have built a reservation for ethnologists in the heart of Africa, where they are protected and maintained in ideal ecological survival conditions and fed at set times of day as is the custom in their countries of origin. The reservation is off-limits to Africans, whether their intentions be philanthropic, scientific or cannibalistic, for fear of damaging the natural equilibrium of the tribe or endangering its chances of breeding, though matters in this regard are already very precarious. The African states assure us that all possible measures will be taken to save this disappearing race: the crucial thing is that it should be completely isolated from the outside world. The first experiment along these lines had already been attempted years ago by the people of Chad, whom the French government had paid a great deal to carry on holding a certain Mme Claustre, an anthropologist, and whom they had thereby saved from the clutches of the Whites who wished to turn her over to scientific prostitution. This almost accidental event soon resulted in all the West's anthropologists rushing off to African reservations, where they could at last devote themselves to the observation of the only ethnic group worthy of the name – their own. By contrast, upon their approach, all the beasts of the savannahs ran off to take refuge in urban zoos, and the Africans themselves withdrew into their missions, for fear of being devoured by ethnologists who had very rapidly reverted to cannibalism.

The moving moment is the one when a woman takes off her shoes and suddenly becomes smaller before your eyes. She becomes marvellously tiny, and, at the same time, her face changes. She creates intimacy in its most seductive form.

Different levels of atrocity.
A DC–10 crashes in the forest of Ermenonville. Three hundred and fifty people are shredded into some twelve thousand pieces. Other societies have accomplished the same thing by other means. Less accidental, bloodier means.

Our atrocity, the one that distinguishes us from everyone else, is the fact of having gathered up all the pieces and run the data through a computer to establish the identity of the dead. To settle the wills and the insurance claims no doubt. But there is something else in play here – the obsessive desire for restoration.

This act – the use of the technology of synthesis to repair the damage wrought by the technologies of death – is what characterizes us. Reassembling the flayed bodies of Ermenonville is of the same order as reconstituting the mummy of Rameses II in a laboratory.

Our atrocity is exactly the reverse of that of earlier centuries. It consists in eradicating the blood and cruelty by use of objectivity. A colourless, programmatic, bloodless atrocity, like the white-noise torture of sensory deprivation cells.

The finest physical and mental exercise: wandering around an unknown town in a certain quality of light. Secret circulation, the virginity of the (nonetheless corrupt) signs of the metropolis, the surprise of the architecture, tiredness, all the senses on the alert, one's body buoyed up by walking, a trance-like state in which all the mechanisms of intuition function at great speed. Catching the town as it emerges, before it has come on stage, leaving the people in abeyance, and their language, which seems oddly familiar to the foreigner ... Then the landmarks awaken from their slumber, meaning is roused, here and there, in fragmentary fashion. But the phase of emergence itself is delicious. Yet, the end has already come. Weariness wins out over the trance.

Paranoiac with fire
Obsessional with the earth
Schizophrenic with water
Hysterical with the winds
All mental ceremonies have an indivisible form.

The passing impulse is now but a mere symptom of the will, all that remains of it in an enervated world.

We are no longer in the era of the will, but of the passing impulse
We are no longer in the era of anomie, but of anomaly
We are no longer in the era of the event, but of the eventuality
We are no longer in the era of virtue, but of virtuality
We are no longer in the era of power, but of potentiality
etc. etc.

The absolution of speed – that of the sleek, ultramodern express train, speeding across the sinister, sooty plains of the North. And there, in your heart, a suspended decision – vital, but impossible to make. Indeed all decisions are suspended, all impulses are accumulating in the firmament. Various different lives awaiting some resolution, the lives of contradictory women. All this is insoluble, but the feline movement of the train still gives it some kind of charm. Railway points are made in our image. Their hearts condense the tenderness of the ironic tracks of the railway.

In an ultravisible, ultrareal, transparent and operational world, one can rely only on silent efficiency.

There is nothing more beautiful than a woman separated from you by a mirror, the mirror of her own hysterical speculation on the world, the mirror of the caresses she spurns and which you overwhelm her with mentally, the mirror of the murder she is planning without realizing it. One must wait patiently for an eternity in front of this mirror which envelops her, haloed as she is by the silvery light of danger. And one day the mirror gives way; it slides like a dress to your feet, leaving before you merely the ashes of hysteria, the vestiges of a woman who has mentally yielded.

There are eyes which make all the miseries to come worthwhile. There are futures which make all previous lives worthwhile, when the woman who has stayed all night also sends you across town.

To Freud: the man who turned pleasure into a principle.
To Lacan: the man who turned the mirror into a phase.

The writers of the Apocalypse were methodical people who preferred to send each other endless letters rather than question the Anti-Christ himself.

Palermo.
The way they drive there conforms to the cruel ceremonial of provocative, animal dancing. It is a challenge verging upon the lethal limit of suicide, but one in which eliding the act preserves the rules of the game. Animals confront each other in this way, to establish supremacy without actually inflicting harm. The violent rhetoric of *hard driving*,* and indeed all the town's scenography are products of this continual dicing with death.
Watching for six centuries over this archaic ceremonial, which sends modern

*In English in original. [Tr.]

19

technology spinning in an endless whirl (at three o'clock in the morning the cars are still tearing around at crazy speeds through this monumental geometric space), there stand, like science-fiction ancestors, the giant, antediluvian fig trees, rhizome-like trees from the mangrove swamps, which are by turns reptilian, visceral, tentacularly mineral, whose sap goes round and round within their networks of stalactite-like branches which reach down to the earth and take root there. Trees without end, neither animal nor vegetable, worthy of some barbarian cult, and of the baroque rootedness of this city in a culture of death.

There is something stupid about raw events of which Destiny, if it exists, cannot be insensible. There is something stupid about self-evidence and truth from which a superior irony cannot but spare us. Thus everything is expiated one way or another. Forgetting or mourning are no more than the period of time required by reversibility.

Clothed woman: obligation to see, prohibition on touching.
Undressed woman: obligation to touch, prohibition on looking.
But this is doubtless something that is changing.

The striated space of life, the smooth space of melancholy. No more plans, neither for loving, nor for writing. That of living remains, like a superficial space in which disparate, fickle objects pass by – all fleeting shapes.

One can make beautiful things simply to get rid of them. Without pride, without vanity – simply by expulsion: I abjure my inertia by acts. These are no more than exorcisms by which I rid myself of the heavy matter of existence.

Nothing done like this could have useful or memorable results. It is simply a question of exhausting life, sex, energy and memory, before it is too late.

With any sort of pain or pleasure, there is the secret desire to get it over with as soon as possible, and the satisfaction of being absolved, for a moment, of existence. The sooner it is over, the longer the absolution.

Bombastic, petty-bourgeois worldview: 'I did what I had to do. Forgive me and get off my back.' Emotionally disturbed worldview: 'I am not responsible, your desire does not affect me, I can do without you.' Worldview of nostalgia: 'The ideal form of existence is an empty one, since that is the form in which some event may chance to cross it at any moment.'

Always lived with men and women of a younger generation. No sense of age difference. Now, all of a sudden, the people I know have started to be 35–40 years old. But instead of feeling they are closer to me, I feel a generation apart. Most people, I think, escape this sudden change in age difference by projecting on to their own children.

Still this naive idea that light, fire and dryness cannot but bring out the finest passions in men, and that the heavy and provincial passions should never have flourished anywhere but in the North and the cold, where they are bound up with some kind of self-preservation instinct. Alas! it is not so, and the whole world, as San Antonio says, is just a little market town.*

*San Antonio (real name Frédéric Dard) is the author and narrator–hero of a series of detective novels. [Tr.]

All life has two trajectories: the one linear and irreversible, the trajectory of ageing and dying, the other elliptical and reversible, a cycle of the same forms in a sequence which knows neither childhood, death nor the unconscious, and which leaves nothing behind. This sequence is constantly intersecting with the other, and occasionally erases all traces of it at a stroke.

Mindless, uncivilized, uncouth, irresponsible, peasant-like, self-centred, unaware, asocial – without reference, without acknowledgement, without allegiance to any form of culture, stranger to any affect, allergic to any kinship. This is the bestial material on which a theory of simulation is built! And on what ignorance of the play of signs and of love a theory of seduction is built! Fortunately, all this is the product of a double life which may have the pathological beauty of writing.

The sovereignty of the object, which has its basis in its lack of desire, coincides with the disappearance of affect in my existence. Eccentricity without affect, far from what we hash up out of a sense of mercy. Radicalism in its sabbatical form.

A new chimaera, born of a combination of a naenia and a fiddler crab, seen from an electric chair and working its way through dubious tear-off calendars.

Only the eyes, the lips and the spoken word cannot be prostituted since these are the organs of divination. It used to be possible to divine the body too, but nowadays it offers divination too simple a solution. It also used to be a diviner, but now it is no more than a carnal form of supply and demand.

All we may expect of time is its reversibility. Speed and acceleration are merely the dream of making time reversible. You hope that by speeding up time, it will start to whirl like a fluid. It is a fact that, as linear time and history have retreated, we have been left with the ephemerality of networks and fashion, which is unbearable. All that remain are the rudiments of a supratemporal peripeteia – a few short sequences, a few whirling moments, like the ones physicists observe in certain particles.

Only one way of looking at things produces a supreme sense of understanding and that is a completely controlled form of delirium or simulation.

Rubik cube: all our thoughts in the wrong order, like the squares on the cube, without ever managing to get all those of the same colour on one side. A devilish, futile game, a fine symbol of the patchwork of magnetic thoughts and the cross-overs between them which make up our world, a world in which we face only insoluble puzzles or useless problems of synchrony.

The imagination is scarcely any better equipped to appreciate reversibility than the person who has never slept would be to appreciate dreaming. And yet we experience it in that electrocution of time we call predestination. The signs exchanged in the process are instant conductors unaffected by the resistance of time. Certain linguistic fragments run back along the path of language and collide with others in the witticism, dazzling reversibility of the terms of language. In this they fulfil an unexpected destiny, their specific destiny as words, conforming to the predestination of language.

Every woman is unique, fragile, ineluctable, immoral, radiant, insatiable. But whether pretty or ugly, she is never any of these things entirely directly. The detour that has to be made runs precisely through the opposite appearance: we have to come to terms with this as we would with the everyday destiny of a fatal vanity.

The whole difference between the sexes resides perhaps not in the way we feel passion for an individual being, but in our feeling of passion for formal abstraction, and the possibility of dying for it, even if it be embodied in a woman.

We have dreamt of every woman there is, and dreamt too of the miracle that would bring us the pleasure of being a woman, for women have all the qualities – courage, passion, the capacity to love, cunning – whereas all our imagination can do is naively pile up the illusion of courage.

We are becoming like cats, slyly parasitic, enjoying an indifferent domesticity. Nice and snug in 'the social', our historic passions have withdrawn into the glow of an artificial cosiness, and our half-closed eyes now seek little other than the peaceful parade of television pictures.

Dying is nothing. You have to know how to disappear.
Dying comes down to biological chance and that is of no consequence. Disappearing is of a far higher order of necessity. You must not leave it to biology to decide when you will disappear. To disappear is to pass into an enigmatic state which is neither life nor death. Some animals know how to do this, as do savages, who withdraw, while still alive, from the sight of their own people.

The beauty of these Japanese tattoos on the thighs of the women: normally invisible, they appear only in the moment of rapture, of lovemaking. A woman is tattooed with the objective marks of her servitude (the tattoo consists of her lover's initials). But what servitude this represents for the lover in return – condemned as he is to arouse this woman, to give her pleasure. If not, she will deny him his initials. The game of passion becomes more difficult. And what a delight for the unknown but well-chosen lover who sees his name appear upon his beloved's body as he makes love to her!

When nothing moves you any more, you must find a sign to stand in for passion.

When nothing is at stake any more, you must find a rule to stand in for necessity.

I have played at passion, I have played at tenderness.

I have played at parting, I have played at sadness.

I have gone as far as I can in expressing sadness, as previously I had gone as far as I could in the appearance of seduction. Sometimes it even seems to me that I have never done anything but provide the semblance of ideas. But that is the one and only way out we have to take in a speculative world with no way out: to come up with the most successful signs of an idea.

Or in an emotional world with no way out: to come up with the most successful signs of a passion.

And I held beneath my eyelids the sweet hologram of her nakedness.

The curvature of things is their only memorable aspect, but you never see it. There are really two forms of speculation, one of which excludes all forms of memory and objective signification.

All the objects, places and faces that are so much a part of us that they intensify our loneliness and we are forced to love them because there will be no others after them. They have involuted into us and we into them; they have created around us the optical illusion of everyday life. At most they are capable, like a mirror, of inverting the symmetry of our lives.

It is quite some time now since all spectacles crashed through the stupefaction barrier. What could be funnier than these armies, which for thirty years have been training on the spot, in the empty space of war? This is the perfect example of simulation, the prototype of a species which has attained perfection in its pointless attributes and which dreams, at great expense, of its virtual destruction (which is, as it happens, thoroughly unlikely).

All individual strains of melody are drowned out by the bass continuo, in which a beat grows stronger, a heartbeat nearing the point of collapse. The inner squinting at one's feelings has now given way to an intent concern with inner sounds, the sounds of the body, like a perpetual tom–tom on tape.

Revenge? Revenge? Everything comes back by itself, very precisely; and revenge confuses it.' (Canetti)*

*Elias Canetti, *The Human Province*. [Tr.]

The same goes for passion: the attraction of beings and things, their violent and material inclination, is so inescapable that passion only confuses matters. And truth? Truth itself only complicates the workings of the mind.

The immateriality of signs is alien to me, as it is to a race of peasants with whom I share an obsessional morality, a sluggishness, a stupid, ancestral belief in the real. In reality, I am one of them.

The simulation hypothesis is merely a maximalist position. The seduction hypothesis is merely a formal abstraction. It is the phantom of seduction which obsesses me – as for the rest, I have never managed anything other than to let myself be seduced. And this is quite alright: all the rest is merely destructive, moral passion.

The seducing monk dreams of a manichean tension between the sign and the real as the most sublime form of morality. Only from time to time, the earth-shattering, hypothetical union of the two . . . Even then, the beauty of this violent resolution eludes him.

Faith and fury first attack the impossibility of believing; they attack signs. Annihilating the world as sign, in order to make it an object of belief.

The people vehement, the beasts silent, the sky grey and luminous. Land of bucolic deceit and wretchedness. The sea does not make the same sound here at night as it does in the West, and this land's festivals are dictated by the moon – that soft roe of a moon – which is like the virile, suffering ideality of Islam.

Animals maintain the nomadic way of life in the very heart of domesticity. Motionless, in their thousands, on the sandy slopes, the arid pasturelands. Yet, animals know no boundaries. The sterile, patriarchal expanses are their world. It is they who order the world of men.

A universe without animal space, without the servile regularity of beasts, is never the same again. It is a long time since we knew such a thing in Europe. It needs a semidesert space, without the marks of property, without demarcation lines. It was by marking out all spaces that we got rid of the desert and of hierarchical servility, which is respectful of the inhuman and takes its orders from the inhuman – from a distant planet or an animal god, the constellations or an imageless divinity. It is a marvellous conception this imageless divinity: nothing could be more opposed to our modern iconolatry.

The gods can only live and hide in animals, in the sphere of silence and objective brutishness, not in the sphere of men, which is that of subjective brutishness, language and psychology. The Man–God is an absurdity. A god who rejects the ironic mask of the inhuman, who steps out of the animal metaphor, in which he was the silent embodiment of the principle of evil, and affords himself the luxury of a soul and a face, at the same time takes on the hypocritical psychology of the human. The gods have to be able to move like animals from one pasture to another. The dividing up of the land was the only way of banishing them.

She had the heavy breath of insomniacs' mouths, the chapped lips of hysterical women, the confused sex of sterile women, and sadness, inexorable sadness. What wouldn't you have given her in her innocence? Neither God, nor pleasure – grace perhaps, the savage grace of felines on the defensive, the retractile grace of her claws and of a gooseflesh extraordinarily soft to the touch, the grace of a fragile and defenceless frame. Nobody can do anything for her. She is impossible to protect, but her whole vulnerability is a caress and her retractility is a weapon, whilst her body, the whole of her body, becomes all weak and sly in order to seduce you.

I call that woman a slut who is capable of shying away from you out of sheer perversity, without any amorous necessity, out of the pure temptation to slip through your fingers. Women are sluts more through this ability to be absorbed hysterically by absence, than by physical and mental prostitution. And I recognize and admire this skill at escaping which is given only to those who do not know the obstacle of value judgements.

For his part, the male is rendered fragile by the mechanisms of representation. He does not have the ability to retract himself so suddenly and absolutely – he has to cast off his image. A woman, on the other hand, may convert herself into an absence by pure reflex or stratagem and surprise a man in that way as cruelly as she may enchant him by her presence.

The story of the ship built with such a quantity of iron and steel that its compass-needle, instead of showing north, simply pointed towards its own mass. Turning endlessly back upon itself, it was eventually lost in the fossilized ice of the Quaternary.

The real joy of writing lies in the opportunity of being able to sacrifice a whole chapter for a single sentence, a complete sentence for a single word, to sacrifice everything for an artificial effect or an acceleration into the void.

The only revolutionary transformation in things today comes not from their dialectical transcendence, but from raising them to the power of x, whether it be the revolution of terrorism, irony or simulation. It is not dialectics that are happening today, but ecstasy. Thus terrorism is an ecstatic form of violence, the state an ecstatic form of society, pornography the ecstatic form of sex, the obscene the ecstatic form of the scenic and theatrical, etc. It seems things have lost their finality and critical determination and can only repeat themselves in their exacerbated, transparent form. This is the case with Virilio's 'pure war': the ecstasy of unreal war, potential and omnipresent. Even space exploration is a *mise en abyme* of this world. Everywhere the virus of virtualization and self-reflexivity is on the upsurge, carrying us on towards an ecstasy which is also the ecstasy of indifference.

*Carnal silence**

Hunger a muted drum of the body devouring the fleshly silence of the Siberian night.

The thrill of existing anywhere vertically above the Urals. The night and its orbit: night itself is an object lost in space – a movement of circular lips and a round of fossilized sound.

This imaginary line running from North to South, where it only takes one step to pass from one day to the next at the same hour – why was it placed in the middle of the Pacific, where only fish, ships and storms are allowed to cross it?

Are there spiritual forms which pass through us in this same way and can we cross them mentally?

You would go mad if you could never forget that the simultaneity of all points on the globe is only a dream or even if you considered the night to be a local object in orbit, which you can cross in any direction.

Intercontinental flight is a mental Odyssey.

The real desert, and therefore real enchantment, is to be found at an altitude of 30,000 feet, where the earth shows in its blue, geological light, like an inhuman essence without any other distinguishing features than the meandering path of its rivers or its mineral undulations, and where time stands perfectly still if you are

---

*In English in original. [Tr.]

lucky enough to be flying in the same direction as the sun.

All their gestures imply that they regard you as precious. Since that is impossible, there isn't even any subterfuge involved. This is true courtesy.

They welcome you as if you were sent by the gods. In the West, you are welcomed as if you were sent by death. In the West, the Other always comes from amongst the dead and has to win the favour of the living. But this continual self-effacement is also a strategy: it leaves you in a horrible state of uncertainty as to whether you should simply succumb to the consideration shown to you or else give even more, i.e. assume the divine role of reciprocation.

It's a contest to see who will have the last smile, the last gesture, the ultimate refinement – a bidding contest, as in poker, and one which raises the same cruel doubt in your mind that you have never given enough or gone far enough. It is a confrontation that can end only in death. For this dual form of exchange is limited by no contract and, as it is not based on culpability, no psychology can help you escape it.

Long after what had to be said has been said and the question of meaning has disappeared, the Japanese know you still have to put an end to signs and exemplary appearances: this is what courtesy is for, that quality which is as artificial as the tormented bonsai trees, that are cared for as though they were thousand-year-old works of art.

Eroticism comes from the same exemplary finishing touches, the perfecting of features, including the features of the face, the vivacity of passion in the slightest gesture, holding out the promise of the same vivacity in sex and pleasure.

To be lively and docile at the same time is a gift possessed only by a painted face or the smooth sex of a doll. The whole race seems to be wearing make-up and smooth as a sex, while retaining its animal vivacity and its restrained violence. When an entire race presents the same distinguishing features, the same ritualism, the same artificial smile, then there is something *sexually* extraordinary in this.

The seductiveness of Japan is the seductiveness of a whole race. It is that of the final touch, the touch of perfection. Sex is no longer then the play of difference and its absorption in pleasure, but the last touch which sanctifies the racial beauty of the eyes, the vivacity of the limbs, the inevitable mirror of the smile.

The statue at Nara, the most beautiful one.

The one of the woman whose hand, attached to the jar which she is barely holding, falls delicately towards the ground, whilst the other is raised in offering to the sky. A double movement, echoed by the hermaphroditism of the statue: the right profile looks masculine, with the elbow raised, while the other is feminine, with the arm hanging down loosely, an aerial form of gravity. As for the body, it is perfectly upright, like the statues at Chartres, but nonetheless sensual thanks to the subtle inflection of forms beneath the silk. All this is inhumanly elongated and produces a strange impression. What is the secret of a statue like this in other than aesthetic terms?

She: a principle of equilibrium in her mental and affective aloofness – absent gentleness.

He: a form of hypochondriacal self-devouring – the recrimination of the body.

What is deeply ingrained within us is this possibility of expecting everything from someone at each new meeting. In our own minds, we are all virgins and hope, against all good sense, to find a destiny in any face that comes along.

The carnal urge to accomplish certain obsessional gestures or improper acts at irregular intervals is only ever characteristic of a second-rate libertine. The true obsessional or libertine has to accomplish them at a set hour.

A carnal horizon has appeared, that of the sex of . . . Like every horizon, this one is an imaginary line where the sun sometimes sets in a blaze of colour and sometimes just gives off a hazy glow.

Innocence, which consists in not even having a glimmer of an idea of the law, is doubly impossible today, since even transgression is improbable.

Appearance, which consists in not even having a glimmer of an idea of meaning, is doubly absent today, since even meaning is dissolving into indifference.

On every level, we are doubly held in check. Our indifference is that of one abyss overlaying another. We have then to find not only a simple act of transcendence but a double inversion. We have to accomplish at a single stroke the two revolutions which can save us from this double disappearance.

Have you ever seen a fly buzzing around on a ceiling?

Why does it always choose to fly in the middle of the room, beneath an absent chandelier? And who dictates this tireless, spasmodic flight, the domestic version of molecular motion? Flies have no understanding of corners. What a mystery! They also have no notion of infinity. They always cover the same tiny space, following a haphazard, secretly depolarized trajectory. They seem also quite ignorant of the notion of equilibrium: they don't seem bothered by several hours of uninterrupted flight in which they amuse themselves with the game of passing through all the points in space: they always know where they have landed and are always ready to set off again. All these senseless movements and circumvolutions seem to have nothing whatever to do with the problems of energy. Unless they draw their energy from repetition itself, from the scrupulous charting of empty insect space, the angular, Lilliputian, Brownian space of the insect from which man, with his inability to move through a right angle, must inevitably seem a monstrous, antediluvian presence.

By comparison with our ideas of liberation, emancipation and individual autonomy, which exhaust themselves chasing their own shadows, how much more subtle, and proud at the same time, is the idea, which still survives in oriental wisdom, that someone else has control over your life, is planning it, determining it, satisfying it, according to the terms of an electoral pact by which you agree to stand down, when things are going against you, from something which, in any case, does not belong to you and which it is much more pleasant to enjoy without constantly having to take responsibility for it at every waking moment. There is nothing to prevent you, in return, from looking after someone else's life – something people are often more skilled at than looking after their own – and so on, from one person to the next, with each of us being relieved of the burden of living, truly free and no longer exposed to their own madness, but only to the ritual or romantic intervention of the other in the process of their own life.

The ultimate achievement is to live beyond the end, by any means whatever.

The difference between things and words is that the real evolves whereas language mutates. Something in language does not function in continuity with things: things go their own way but, at a given moment, a particular word takes on a specific meaning, and it loses it just as unexpectedly. Certain things also appear or disappear without further ado, pass from one state to another surprisingly, discontinuously, though this is not the discontinuity of chance, but that of another kind of necessity. Our lives thus have two wavelengths. On the one, plans and events follow logically. On the other – crazy – curve, the same events recur ceaselessly. The same crime can keep happening forever throughout an entire dynasty, the same tic may persist right through to your grandchildren. In one of your lives, you are going in a straight line; in the other, you are going round in circles. When the two lines cross, it is an absolutely critical moment. When they coincide, it is the solstice of happiness.

Technology evolves, language changes, the voice breaks, fate overtakes us.

Naming things is never innocent. It is to precipitate them beyond their own existence into the ecstasy of language which is already the ecstasy of their end.

We have no more reasons to exist than stones and if one part of our life is in the sun, then, necessarily, the other is in the cold of hell.

It is through animal sensations such as running your tongue over your lips or your hand over your eyes that you get a sense of the truth of sexual difference.

Who ordered the sexes to differ, and not to alternate like the seasons or to follow one another as night follows day? When the sexes are in opposition to one another in the same way as occurs with planets, i.e. when they are in perpetual ellipsis on each other's horizons, then the vanity of all sexual liberation will become glaringly obvious.

The individual, floating, but held on a leash like a dog, like an eye popping out of its socket, hanging on the end of its optic nerve, scanning the horizon through 180 degrees but not sending back any images – a disembodied panoptical terminal, runaway organ of a species of mutants.

The body ought to learn to develop the figures of slow motion, of suspense, stopping, fixity, slowness. We are experts in the figures of acceleration but inexpert at instantaneously arresting movement, as animals can, or as happens in ceremonies (in the Peking Opera, movement does not die away through inertia but always comes to a perfect stop, a perfect climax in immobility).

Look at the difficulty gymnasts have controlling their landings. Even the best of them get it wrong, but this is what it's really all about, because as a gymnast cannot come to a climax of weightlessness at the highest point of his movement through the air, he must be able to produce the equivalent of this on the ground, in the ecstasy of landing. The ground must absorb all his energy (that is the secret of cats). Either you can bounce back up completely or you can break your fall entirely, get rid of all your inertial energy and come to an immediate stop, like a noise absorbed without echo (what fascinates us in the colour black, in the black body is this idea of a total absorption of light, which is equivalent to the dizziness of immobility for the body).

This art of absorbing energy without giving it back, suspending a movement without falling back, escaping those prolongations which give our bodily processes a certain gracelessness is also the art of slow motion and its tragic effect. We have given up that slowness for the prestige of acceleration.

The only role that has fallen to women is that of a sacred prostitution. A radical devotion accompanied by a desperate absence. Just once a woman has to have materialized in your life as if from another world and said 'I love you', and you have to have welcomed her without even knowing her name. Once in your life an idea or a phrase has to have come to you as if in a dream and have immediately taken possession of you. For, if language is to seduce or strike your imagination, words themselves also have to have indulged in a sacred form of prostitution. These are the only gestures of affection a blind destiny can show towards us.

Only ideology has prestige in the fashionable world, because it alone is combatted. And yet there are more serious ideas which have no visible enemy.

Indifference of the sky to the earth: it will not rain
Indifference of the soul to things: it will not mingle with them
Indifference of lips to words: they maintain their silence
Indifference of dreams to reality: they will not absolve it

The hysterical obsession with events is itself a result of the end of history. Since there is no longer any history, events should follow one another in endless succession. Since there are no longer any causes, effects must be produced without any break in continuity. Since there is no more meaning in anything, everything should function perfectly.

Against the whole controversy about chance.
Determinism, indeterminism?
What use is there in establishing that chance is an objective process when it is in fact an ironic process? Certainly it exists, but only as the pataphysics of causes and effects, and fate exists as well, at the same time. The difference is that the irony of fate is greater than the irony of chance, which makes it both haughtier and more seductive.

Here begins my delirious self-criticism (all self-criticism is delirious, the worst form of the critical spirit being that which claims to be directed against itself). Nonetheless, I accuse myself of:

– having surreptitiously mixed my phantasies in with reality and, more precisely, with the little amount of reality available at this most mediocre moment in history
– having systematically opposed the most obvious and well-founded notions, in the hope that they would fall into the trap of this radicalism, which has not occurred
– having dreamt of a different world which – whether women or concepts – would have been that of a sacred form of prostitution
– having subtly drawn my energy from the energy of others according to a mental law of derivation
– having cultivated a twilight zone of thought the more effectively to disguise the difference between night and day
– never having been tempted to throw everything away, but merely obsessed by a sense of frustration and of having sublimated all cowardice in theoretical radicalism
– having sinned by omission of references

AMEN

Of being profoundly carnal and melancholy

Of having withdrawn from things to the extent that any judgement I make is merely the word of a phantom

But where are the blinding insights of yesteryear? Around me I see nothing but groundless hysteria and unscrupulous vitality

AMEN

Two inalienable skins rigged out in opposing kinds of cynicism and considered as masks. Respect for the mask. Submission to unlimited reciprocal judgement. Total commitment and total egoism: distances are kept.

The final implied effusion is like a last judgement. Meanwhile, meticulous precautions are taken towards the mask, which is not a function of presence, since this is unceasing and haunts us like a slow-burning, indirectly fuelled flame. No longer any distinction between body and soul, but only between created things such as the colour of eyes. And yet, a painstaking and persistent hostility.

Proximity hostility tension distance.

The distance between soul and mask is maintained by a lengthy apprentice-ship to work up their silences into a proper duel.

The atmosphere also involuntarily affected by what surrounds them and denying this to each other in a judgement long since silently adapted to the dissimulation of people and animals. In everything – distance, complicity, hostility, judgement – the same schema within one's self, within the other – and within all the rest, which is judged in terms of this.

Constantly lying in wait. Constant fear that the other may have switched allegiances one day and that their judgement of what is good and bad may have altered. Because their intervention is fundamental in the most important questions. Yet I resolve these by myself. And he is different and leaves me feeling lonely. This is the way a duel suzerainty of understanding comes about. When we clash, it is to train our two shadows to coincide. When we agree, it is because we have judged on our own. The two cynicisms must be properly differentiated.

The complicity in all this is so precious that it seems to creep around on tiptoe and to be ashamed of and superstitious about itself, recognizing that it represents the highest court of judgement in both our cases: he is judged and so am I; there can be no escape. That is why this complicity keeps such a watch on itself and avoids its own reflection, because it is aware of itself as an imaginary solution, and not the only one possible.

OCTOBER   1 9 8 1

Bright, icy sunshine like moonlight on snow or the tragic cry of seagulls over the green sea of a February twilight.

The choice would be between a woman who would be happy to give you an assurance of uninterrupted sexual potency (and where does this sensual genius come from in a woman?) and a woman so mentally enigmatic as to frighten off the slightest caress.

Accumulation is a paralytic's dream. When you accelerate, everything starts swirling around.

There is a particular kind of provocative moodiness which has something of the daydream about it, something of the defiant gesture of loving without being loved or of any kind of intense feeling so long as it is willing to take everything and to sacrifice itself, which can only be compared to a sort of ether, a mental elixir, a firing of the nerve-ends and the elation of an intelligence happy in its own duplicity. A woman in such a state is so beautiful you have to seduce her. The world in such a state is so beautiful you have to destroy it.

What one dreams of is a beautiful, formal style of thinking, which despairs of its object clearly and takes its revenge without hypocrisy, by pulling aside the veil of jealousy.

If you don't have to be missed by someone, it is no use slipping away
If you do not have to love her, it is no use being missed by her
If you do not have to destroy her, it is no use loving her

What else was it that charmed me if not that passionate affection, which I have only ever been able to absorb, without being able to reciprocate? I lacked passion when it mattered, but she too lacked originality when it mattered.

Jealousy gets the same results as passion, but it gets them cold, like in a dream. Might it be the basic passion of the age of psychology, that is, of a fate always deferred and indifferent? For psychology itself is only a belated perception of the obvious.

Every man has an intense fear that he will no longer be taken in charge by some woman or female image. No one can live without the absolution of a female image.

Brilliant little irruptions
Brilliant little connections
Brilliant little illusions
Brilliant little lips
Brilliant little altercations
Very brilliant little honeycombs
Brilliant little adversities
Very brilliant little ravages
Brilliant little cogs
Brilliant little circumvolutions
             around a vertical axis

Why has the deficiency of the mentally deficient become a cultural fact, whereas the very much more terrible fact of ordinary stupidity strikes no one as very odd?

Moscow Airport. Bureaucratic stupidity knows no bounds once it has aestheticized itself in the performance, once it is raised to the aesthetic power of a cold-war rhetoric. A cold war waged by the state against each citizen, all the more odious for being artificially sustained. A simulacrum of stupidity which has become the only vehicle of social life. A whole society with its eyes popping out beneath the mask of military power, a whole civil society reduced to blandness beneath the mask of bureaucracy. A dead society, clinging on to the appearance of death, to a final performance which it cultivates as a bitter denial of its own reality.

The only historical advantage that comes from Soviet society is that certain characteristics, certain customs of the human race will be found saved and preserved there, as mammoths were saved by the ice age, when they will have disappeared everywhere else.

The workers, once the heroes of historical negativity, have become the transparent unemployed workforce of factories that are but simulacra. The intellectual, once the herald of historical negativity, has become the transparent clown of dissidence.

Bureaucracy had found the best way of exploiting cadaveric rigidity in the social world. We found something better: cadaveric flexibility which had already been adopted by the efficient Jesuits, supple as corpses, helping grace to flow in worldly circles. Today electronics has replaced grace; it circulates in the semi-tetanic, semifluid networks of the immense and flexible mortification system which serves as our driving force. And the same jesuitical strategy, indifference, works a treat there.

The insomniac dreams of a loss of consciousness, which would allow him to sleep; in the same way, the acrobat dreams of a failure of gravity, which would allow him never to fall again.

You can dream of a theory which would work like acupuncture, by the faintest touching, by an unexpected correlation of sensitive spots over a distance, using its gold needles to create short-circuits across them.

In any system there must be a nerve centre which, if you touch it in some way, causes the whole system to contract and implode, as with a crystalline solution, just as, when a particular spot in the brain is touched, it immediately plunges the body into sleep.

There must be a somnambulic lucidity which allows you to go right to the heart of things just as there must also be a particular position of the body which would put you to sleep instantly.

When the force of love is spent, there comes the serenity of the state of weakness. When the crime has been committed, there comes the serenity of expiation. In all things, one should only concern oneself with the effects and leave the causes to the Last Judgement.

Hegel: the injustice of society is that it is the subordinate who has to understand what power is.

Aristotle: all organic existence proceeds from two sources – on the one hand, from its natural causes and, on the other, from the necessary intervention of the sun.

I have the impression – more or less – that this abject and glorious mercenary has a dual nature, that she is torn between the two sides of the same character – Leo rising in Leo – time alone, or depressive illness being able to distinguish in her heart between the two rivals, who in reality are only one. In mythological terms, I see this creature of the sea undulating like a suicidal Aphrodite between two opposite poles, fleeing on an invisible wire as far as the luminous escarpment of the lower world, where lurks the touching brute who will kill her.

In astral terms, I see the pendulum in her heart hesitating like a metronome out of kilter – magnetic hesitation of the needle between two signs, femininity floating in the double helix of the will to power.

Sublime epigraph on seduction in Omar Khayyam:

'It is better for you to have reduced a single free man to slavery by gentleness than to have freed one thousand slaves.'

Organic and sepulchral mystery of concupiscence.
Crucial and imponderable universe of concomitance.
Alleluia!

Only cats leave the total imprint of their sleeping bodies on the sand or the
bed. Man does not know how to abandon himself to the form of his body, so as to
experience total abandon. He does not know the inertia from which the cat draws
its felinity, its vivacity, its formal cruelty. He does not know that mystic elasticity,
the dissolution of the body into its various members, which enables the cat to fall
without being crushed as it lands. For in itself each part is light; it is the heaviness
of the whole which is our perdition.

Why did we have to leave the perfect, silent indifference of the plant
kingdom? Why did we have to abandon the immobility of the mineral kingdom,
the swiftness of the animal kingdom? In man, the metamorphosis reaches its end.
Yet the animals still speak to us of it: a cat, a horse, a bird, an octopus, what are
these forms unintelligible to human understanding but the signs of a lineage
whose powers of fabulation end with our species?
    But perhaps women retain something of this enigma, something of the
immobility and swiftness.

The mental dread of the tree with ice-laden branches
the paradoxical dread of the woman disrobed
the mental dread of the naked truth
the paradoxical dread of the waking dream

When the night is as long as the day, then the storms of the equinox begin to get up, when artificial light is as strong as the violence of the sun, then the passion for gambling is unleashed, when two women equal each other in your mind, then the equinox of pleasure begins.

For some, life is interminable, and what is interminable no longer makes sense. How are they to find time to live? For others, life is over right from the outset. It has ended before it has begun. It unfolds on a sort of abstract strip, without any temporal dimension. In this way, some lives sacrifice their own ends uselessly, and lose even the memory of their origins.

If there were a secret, no one, not even the person who knew it, would be able to divulge it.

We must keep watching, from the depths of a definitive silence, for the definitive event.

There is, on the one hand, a crazy world, and, standing over against it, nothing but the ultimatum of realism. This means that if you want to escape from the folly of the world, you must also sacrifice everything of its charm. By increasing its delirium, the world has raised the cost of the sacrifice. It's a blackmailing by reality. Today, to survive, illusions are no use any more; you must get closer and closer to the nullity of the real.

The repetition of days is interminable, that of nights less so. It is probable that the succession of nights has a meaning, whereas that of the days leads us nowhere. The day should simply break, and then immediately come to an end. Things should just appear, and be immediately abolished.

The loss of virile mythologies, and also of feminine emblems, with the concomitant rise of a transsexual, narcissistic mirage common to both sexes, which only falsely assumes an air of homosexuality.

The seductive power of the feminine bends back on itself. As for men, they can only have recourse to the mirror of woman, but this is already occupied.

Pompeii: we are indebted to a catastrophe for having preserved the most extraordinary piece of our classical heritage. But for Vesuvius we would not have had this living hallucination of Antiquity. As we owe the preservation of mammoths to the sudden onset of the Ice Age. Today, it is all our artificial memory systems that play the museum-building role of natural disasters.

At male stripshows, it is still the women that we watch, the audience of women and their eager faces. They are more obscene than if they were dancing naked themselves. This is so because of the hysterical overflow from their sexes into their faces, but particularly because what they are looking for is a right of revenge over men. What is obscene more than anything else in all this is the egalitarian demand for the right to pleasure.

No one has any right to pleasure, any more than to water or to life. Let us leave this form of legality to the emancipated slaves. Enjoying life has already been rendered obscene by the right to leisure. This time it is sex that is being rendered obscene by the right to sexuality. Obscenity threatens everything that claims to be considered as a legal right.

The right to pleasure and the right to suffering usher in a civilization of hysteria and gaudy vulgarity. The ecstasy of the female strip clients is akin to the ecstasy of the holy women of Lisieux. The same form of voracity is directed towards the masculine sex or the Sacred Heart of Jesus.

The body on stage is never obscene. The only thing that is is the cannibalistic gaze of these women absorbed in their own symbolic revenge and the living derision of their sex. Man is a touching sight in his contemplative pornography (peep show, live show, etc.). He confusedly pays homage with his gaze to the perfection of a body which lacks nothing. For men do not believe in this business of the castrated woman. They know woman has a perfect body and that her body will never lack anything. And their gaze reflects this: if the feminine body can offer itself naked in this way, deliver itself up to the eyes without withholding anything, this is the sign of a great power. The power of prostitution which man will never know, any more than he will know that of parturition.

Whereas what women come to look at in a masculine striptease is precisely castration. Deep down, they are the only ones who really believe in it. That is why the gaze has no option but to turn back upon them, these women who are madly keen on castration and who have become the impure subjects of castration, instead of shining forth as pure objects, in their nudity, with their powers of illusion, on the pornographic stage of the body.

*Female mud wrestling**
The female in *Quest for Fire. Goldfinger*
*Sweet Movie:** the woman in liquid chocolate
Natives in their masks of mud

*In English in original. [Tr.]

51

Blacks with glistening skins
Bodies greased with suntan oil on the beaches.

The lubricious is that which is lubricated. Which slides. Which looks like a sex emerging from a sex, or a child emerging from its mother. When the skin puts on show the inside of the body, with its mucous membranes turned inside out, the moistness of sexual arousal.

A sweating body already offers a show of erotic repulsion and attraction. The body's primordial temptation to cover itself with its secretions. A mere trickle of water flowing over a smooth stone is enough to make it erotic. Everything that slides evokes sexual pleasure, even the wind. Why not oil or mud?

The body in its liquid form is life itself. The opposite of *Goldfinger*, in which it dies transfixed within its film of gold.

But the fluid must not be too fluid. It is the viscosity of mud which gives pleasure, even one's gaze slides and becomes viscous. Sliding would thus seem to be the source of all pleasure, and perhaps of meaning.

In just one week, winter, spring and summer following one after the other. Hence the dreamy mists of the St Lawrence, caused by the tepid rain falling on the ice. On the other side of the lake, the Indian village takes on the dramatic form of the Great North, of exile and snow. But here, in the city, everything takes on the dramatic form of ennui. There are two forms of energy in Montreal, the electric energy of the Great Lakes and the psychological energy of monotony.

There is a vigorous and a languid way to conduct politics. The same applies to lovemaking. The conjunction of the two styles produces the best effects and the best-looking children.

This is the secret of a life: how many faces and bodies would you recognize by caressing them with your eyes closed? From whom would you accept anything with your eyes closed? Have you yourself ever closed your eyes, have you ever acted blindly, have you loved blindly and sensed, in the dark, the tactile windings of ideas?

Seduction is the direct and murderous irradiation of the object, the end of metaphor, the strategy of an enchanted world, the triumphant resurrection of an illusion which puts an end to the dialectical swoonings of sense and the all too naive ruses of history.

If you wish to speak of fiction, the text must obliterate all reference. If you are speaking of simulation, the text must scoff at meaning, while at the same time being completely true. If you are speaking of seduction, language has to pervert something or other in elliptical ways. Otherwise, what would language be there for?

Language is a woman: it seduces you by metamorphosing into what it says. It is a woman also in that it will never stop taking its revenge if it does not succeed in seducing you. It will avenge itself by saying only what you make it say, like a woman who only satisfies what you ask of her.

The Suicide Academy: you go there to take refresher courses in will power. Which is indeed a very academic subject. In the Suicide Motel (a project never fulfilled in the grandiose form in which it was conceived) the verdict of the client who comes to hire the motel's services is irrevocable. He is not given back any free choice (this would be to do him scant honour!). Wine, women and philosophy, etc., are lavished upon him. But, on the appointed day, he is executed, in accordance with his own wishes, in what are the best conditions for him.

That face. Even in ten years' time, I shall still not know the colour of its eyes. But I see it in the street, in my dreams and just beneath the surface of a great number of other faces which suddenly start to resemble it.

The panic of coming upon a transvestite in the Bois de Boulogne. It is not the spectre of homosexuality, but the distortion of signs that spreads terror. Not the fact of mistaking one sex for another, which is close to vaudeville, but the game of signifying woman out of nothing, the signs of woman without woman.

Only the feminine can surrealize its effects in this way without bringing upon itself that ridicule which immediately threatens masculine values when they attempt the same. Besides, the masculine version of the transvestite has become passé; it was merely an appendage of homosexuality.

It is obvious that a woman will always know better how to caress another woman than any man will. This is true, no doubt, of the other sex too. Each sex would thus be like a particular species and the caress a kind of basic language peculiar to the species.

There is no point in building. There is no more real estate, no more life annuities. There are no more concessions in perpetuity in any cultural cemeteries. Isn't it better that way? When a meteorite breaks up in space, it is the dazzling trace of its end which stands out. With a celestial body in orbit, it is the ellipse that is the most precious. No ancestors, no heritage, no heirs, no capital. For centuries we have had to accumulate. It is equally obvious that we have to squander everything in a single generation.

The future belongs to those who have accumulated everything, then un-burdened themselves of it in a single lifetime. You have to move quickly. Ten years to soak up a culture, twenty years to expel it, spew it out (this part always takes longer). Nothing is interesting unless it passes through the entire cycle of the symbolic murder of culture.

The ultimate bomb, the one no one talks about, would be the one which, not content simply to disperse things in space, would disperse them in time. The temporal, palinodic, anachronistic bomb. When it explodes everything is thrown back into the past and, the more powerful the bomb, the further back it is thrown. Or better still, when it explodes some fragments are thrown into the past, others into the future.

But just take a look around: this explosion *has already occurred.* There is no bomb which hasn't already exploded before being technologically invented: the real is always ahead of technology and war. In a world without memory like ours, everything is already projected live into the past; it is as if things had been pre-cipitated into a dimension where they have no meaning other than when they are fixed by a definitive revolution of time.

That, in fact, is the real bomb, the one which immobilizes things in a spectral recurrence. All you can hope for is that some fragments – aeroliths or meteorites – may have passed into the dimension of the future where we will run into them one day with a sense of déjà-vu.

The nuclear is like revolution. Nothing is gained from hoping for the one or fearing the other, since both *have already happened.* Everything is already liberated, changed, subverted. What more do you want? There's no use hoping: the things are there, born or stillborn, already in the past – it's exasperating, but what can you do about it? No future. No cause for panic either: everything's already nuclearized, enucleated, vaporized. The explosion has already happened, the bomb is only a metaphor. What more do you want: everything is already *wiped off the map*. It's no good dreaming: the confrontation has already happened, quietly, everywhere. Yet it isn't enough for things to have happened: we also want to see them happen as spectacle. As we know, the revolution had already taken place within things, before it broke out as spectacle. The people wanted the *spectacle* of the revolution. Things themselves also want to experience the rapture of a spectacular metaphor. This is the revenge of the objectivity in which we have confined them.

What will become of the nuclear? Will we insist on having the grand spectacle of the atomic confrontation for the beauty of it? If that happens, it will not be for the reasons currently advanced – the fatal dynamic of the *use-value* of weapons or the species becoming resigned to its own destruction – but from the irresistibility of the *spectacle* of destruction and the necessity, for us, of deriving some enjoyment from it.

The only response to the missiles: decoys and simulation. An aircraft carrier, a nuclear power station, a simulated metropolis with the same mass, the same potential energy and the same temperature profiles – ultimately every target could surround itself with an infinite number of decoys serving as a protective halo. This was Numa's idea, when, as king of Rome, he had twelve identical shields made in order to prevent the original sacred one sent by the gods from being stolen.

The fact is that the universe was like this in the beginning: undecided as to the authenticity of things. Out of the twelve shields were born the twelve kingdoms and no one knows which is the real one, nor – subtle perfidy of Numa – if there ever was a real one.

If war did break out, it still isn't clear why the missile would choose to hit the decoy rather than the target? Only a man, a conscious being who has passed through the mirror phase, would almost unfailingly choose the decoy (the power of seduction!). But won't a machine, which is an artifact, let itself be lured by the real target? We should therefore be using the most sophisticated military technology we possess to build missiles which are subjects and capable of being lured away by decoys.

It feels so good to disappear among the masses! Even better than getting high on transcendance (God), is to wallow in the nausea of immanence. The Masses. A dream opportunity for the individual to disappear and yet still be able to lament his alienation and his lost subjectivity. Isn't this just what the masses were invented for? Because we did invent them, just as we invented the cold, blue light of television, so that, gazing deep into the screen, we could await the dazzling sign of a definitive event.

To be erotic, the objects of your interest have to be in a state of sexual ease, more dreaming than desiring, lying back nonchalantly, asleep, or miles away, wrapped in some narcissistic concern. They have to have forgotten about you and yet offer themselves to you in some strange way, with a sort of indifferent animality, gentle folly and involuntary nakedness. Only the body without desire is truly deserving of pleasure.

To make you wish to seduce her, a woman should not show herself too inclined toward rape or toward giving herself to you. She must give out not signs of defeat, but of passing weakness, which are so many ways of saying: I am allowing you to seduce me.

The man is dependent on the woman in all this: without this tiny, ultraviolet sign of weakness, he cannot even be tempted to seduce. Perhaps blue eyelashes are this allusive sign, virginal behaviour this fragile allusion. The initiative of seduction always consists in awakening slumbering appearances. And you can guess that a woman will be – or wants to be – seduced by the fact that, as in a lover's snare, she gives herself the appearance of sleep.

She can jettison her existence, her plans and her passions at a single stroke. She is only committed to reality through a secret electoral pact, by which she will stand down if she is losing. She never assumes responsibility for her existence, which allows her to wipe out at a stroke and to slide, like a good hysteric, towards another life. A strange life, spun out entirely towards a goal of transaction. Let a man ask her to give it up, to sacrifice the whole of it, and it all ceases to exist.

The Epeda Multispire mattress. Everyone can have their own night, their own sleep thanks to the 3,600 spiral springs which guarantee everyone complete autonomy. The ideal mattress. You can make love to someone on it without them even noticing. As the automaton of his own pleasure, each person's experience of their sexuality is like their experience of a night on a Multispire mattress. It isn't even loneliness, since there is someone else there. It's more something of the order of the independent lunar module. Tristan and Isolde each dreaming to themselves, on either side of their sexual console.

That seduction is the seduction of the uterine Mother and that all attraction merely masks the attraction of the primal abyss are platonic ideas. The cavity of the womb has taken over from the Cave in the Realm of Ideas. Once again, the real woman, her anatomy, serves as a sacred referent for a platonic ideology. The vertigo of seduction is here vulgarly phantasized into the hollow of a woman's womb. This is to move from the most subtle game to the most profound – and hence the most stupid – phantasm.

Everyday experience falls like snow. Immaterial, crystalline and microscopic, it enshrouds all the features of the landscape. It absorbs sounds, the resonance of thoughts and events; the wind sweeps across it sometimes with unexpected violence and it gives off an inner light, a malign fluorescence which bathes all forms in a crepuscular indistinctness. Watching time snow down, ideas snow down, watching the silence of some aurora borealis light up, giving in to the vertigo of enshrouding and whiteness.

Little catastrophe scenario

I. Losing one's identity papers – your whole being refuses to believe in this, just as it refuses to believe in the death of a loved one. You search for hours before reconciling yourself to the idea, and even then you keep alive a hope of seeing them reappear miraculously, like a woman who has left you. The fact is that they have become your shadow in the sunny world of capital. You are an orphan – and indeed the people who hang around in lost property offices look like shadows themselves. There is a logic in this: the loss of your papers is never innocent, it is a sign of ruination. It is an alarm signal. Many will have been saved in this way from much more serious trouble.

II. Lost passport dream. It turns out to have been true: when I wake up, I can't find it (what would happen if I dreamt I was dead?). The day before, in the search for my identity (papers), I'm told that a passport isn't a true certification of existence, but merely an international transit document. I lost it a quarter of an hour later, and I lost it in the police station, where it remained, like the purloined letter, in full view of everyone.

III. The stolen/non-stolen car. I learn that my own car has been stolen for four years. So they can't give me a vehicle registration document. So I'm driving round in my own stolen car and I have no identity papers. Who am I? The disconnected computer cannot recognize the existence of a real object in the absence of a Search Termination Procedure. But all the documents have disappeared. The unfathomability of machines, the expectancy of men. On the other hand, for the last four years, all traffic offences have been cancelled by the computer because my car was stolen. Moral of the story: it is the art of disappearing that brings total impunity.

IV. In the end, everything turns up again. *Happy end.** I even find myself – reverse catastrophe – with a double identity: two vehicle registration documents, two driving licences, two identity cards, etc.

Ethical hummingbird
Surrealist mercenary
the automaton of one's own pleasure
    a subject without other
            without Other
            without otherness
            without Unconscious
Metamorphosis: only other, then Subject/Other: metaphysics
then only the subject without other: Metastasis
      A past, recycled, narcissistic, refreshed subject
      without transcendence
      paralysed self-fascinated metastatized metastabilized
                                    ecstatic
No Otherness   no alternative
Autarkic nebulosity of subsystems: politics ethnic groups
                   psychic language
No one talks here anymore
No one exists – me included
               Ab-solute centripetal involuted writing

*In English in original. [Tr.]

Then return of the absolute
Other of seduction   of
Surprise and of Rapture

                 Pure event   pure object
                 putting an end to this
introverted and ultimately melancholy fascination
Autorepetition of a subjectivity without desire

Brazil 1982
Equinoctial France. South of the equinox, no more sin.
The little girl from Recife – Salomé.
The sensuality of the plant life, the fruit, the bodies, the poverty – this languorous filth of the Tropics. This slowness of gestures, of thoughts. This Creole unconscious, anthropological and anthropophagic (out of love). How good it must be to eat a bishop on the beach, after mass, after seeing him shipwrecked!

Cannibalistic, amorous, seductive culture. Evil fruits, whose flesh is like the product of a noxious imagination, dull and hairy, obscenely turgescent, having a melancholy freshness.

The favelas that stretch down like glaciers to the edges of the rich quarters. Hanging on the hills, they are waiting to slide, like the earth which will bury the Sheraton beneath the rubble of poverty. But this event itself remains hanging and that is where the beauty of the town lies: for if overcrowding is poverty, the crowding together of poverty and of luxury is the mark of another kind of wealth. Like the intertwining of the mountains and the urbanized zones along the capricious fringes of the sea. Insularity has its role here in the town, as it does out at sea, in the archipelagos.

No discrimination, but no equivalence either, nor equality in difference. The alternative is neither equality of rights nor a fusing together of the races, it is antagonistic seduction, a little like the cannibalistic devouring of a loved one.

Sexual and cultural attraction of the races for one another.

There is nothing more beautiful than a blonde half-caste with blue eyes: the surprise of an illogical conjunction and a purer model.

Seduction plunges us into discrimination as it plunges us into predestination. Day and night do not have to be equals, nor must one race equal another: they must seduce one another.

Brazil is still the land of a baroque mix. Racial puritanism never did get a hold there, but this tropical solution is, perhaps, fragile.

The only austerity here: that of rites, not that of morality, that of observance, not that of repression. A cannibalistic society has no unconscious. It is no more sadistic than the luxuriant vegetation: it devours out of love. Northern sexuality is a form of ostracizing of the world by the body. Equinoctial sexuality is a form of absorption of the world by the body, vegetation, music and dance.

Samba, capoeira.

Neither an explosion of desire, nor a political insurrection. Sympathetic magic. A form of cultural magic which absorbs the other culture, metabolizes it, swallows it up. A stratagem of allegiance and fragility; the European tonal system is destabilized by syncopation; European rationality is absorbed into the fetish, *feiticho*: the fake, the factitious, the decoy, everything that embodies the abominable mixedness of the object and its magical and artificial double. The truth, the purity of the race also suffer syncope, to which is added the indolence of tired bodies. Everything in the term fetish, from the Whites' standpoint, designates the other culture as seduction, a seduction which, in spite of all their material and political power, they find it impossible to resist.

The phantasy these notes cultivate is that they will be read afterwards, elsewhere, after I am gone for good. They may indeed be read as such right now, as a short treatise on the rest of my life. Each thought is the last, each note the final touch, each idea merely appears and disappears, like that planet which is a continuous succession of sunrises and sunsets. They are multiple fragments of a nonexistent hypothetical continuity which can only be rediscovered beneath these notes like a watermark, after death.

The only passion today: the passion for a multiplicity of simultaneous lives, for the metamorphosis and anamorphosis of modes of life, of places, of ways of loving. Every object is unique and should be all that our imaginations require. But there's nothing we can do about it: we have to move on from one to the other. Every landscape is sublime, but there's nothing we can do about it: we have to swap them one for another continually and the sublime today lies in the intercontinental flight which connects them all together. The capacity to pass from one life to another, and not to die in only one life – that beats everything.

Perhaps our eyes are merely a blank film which is taken from us after our deaths to be developed elsewhere and screened as our life story in some infernal cinema or dispatched as microfilm into the sidereal void.

'We prefer the storms of freedom to the silence of servitude.'
A sublime statement, but freedom is no longer stormy today, and servitude no longer silent.
Today, we have the silence of freedom.
In fact, neither freedom nor servitude have any importance these days; the rhetoric of values is dead. Only the storm remains, the storm that lights up real clouds with its flashes of heat, and silence, real silence – the silence of the sky before the storm.

Thirst drives away the dark bile of organic melancholy. The torrid icebergs of

Vingrau, its limestone white as an icefloe in a heatwave, everywhere flowers, thirst: lions were running around here 500,000 years ago in the grasslands; our little regressions do not have this same savage dimension. The rocks, blue like the ice of la Caune de l'Arago, purple, abyssal coolness, mineral liquid melancholy, the purple liquid ecstasy of fatigue. Bestial, prehistoric site midway between sea and hills. Why have men not always lived beside water? For fear of wild beasts, they chose the slopes. For fear of the heat, they chose listlessness. For fear of melancholy, they chose grotesquerie and madness.

None of that has changed very much.

Tautavel, June 1982.

A spider so fragile, so spindly, so translucent that it runs like a watermark across the paper, just like the tiny blood vessels on your skin. It disturbs nothing, running around in the void, in a very great hurry to live and die. In fact, its tiny size, its microscopic structure is a challenge to the monstrous being that we are. Its fragility can only make us wish to crush it, and that would not even be a crime since our two universes are so entirely separate.

To lose the original, but find its double – to lose face, but recover one's image, to lose innocence, but recover one's shadow – then to go through the sunlight to enter the warm night of women, their emotionless gazes, their caressed bodies, their skin made gentle by suffering.

Heat creates a kind of panic extraversion of our perceptions, a sort of social confusion. It discharges us of the burden of our sexuality: our bodies have too much to do to want to reproduce. Sexual pleasure is no longer something obvious, is almost ridiculous. Why add this additional excess? Work and ascesis are both secretions too and sweat is a preferable substitute. It is the moist ecstasy of the body offering itself in reparation to such a sun. There is nothing so good as heat for fusing bodies in a single spasm, in the same archaic abandon. Everything copulates with heat. Irony increases in the sun and the shadow of the subject shrinks. The speed of molecules takes us beyond the point of will power, even the will power needed to cross the road. Heat even cancels out sleep: how can you sleep with this *spectacle* of heat going on? And why sleep anyway, since the heat already offers itself to you like a dream?

Nothing is more liberating than great heat, since when it is hot we give back to the sun all the energy it dispenses to us in a somnambulistic equivalence. We take nothing away for effort and enjoyment; we are merely the mirrors of a thermal equivalence without memory. And this state is more beautiful than that of desire. It is the state the Ancients finely distinguished as the swoon. And then, after all, heat is an alibi for indolence.

There is a perverse stubbornness in preserving a space of ill-will, of rejection of the world and the political order. But also justified aversion for the idea of our collective assumption into the firmament of the operational, of general, simulated reconciliation. We already have too few enemies. In this age of socialist synergy, do we also have to cultivate consensus?

Cowardice and courage are never without a measure of affectation. Nor is love. Feelings are never true. They play with their mirrors. Today it is events which are neither true nor false and which play with their screens. You can no more isolate an event from its screen than in the past you could isolate a passion from its mirror.

There is something archaic in tall buildings and tower blocks heroically defying gravity. It is easier to imagine tower blocks only starting at the fifteenth floor because that is the point where they become interesting. Or even a style of architecture which would begin on the surface of the sky and reach down towards the ground in unequal lunges, and no doubt would not end there. Theory should do the same and start out from the end of things, from their presumed altitude and move back down towards their 'reality', but not even stop there, for that is only an imaginary line.

If we want theory to run on to infinity on both sides of reality, we should knock down the first fifteen storeys right away . . .

Hypothetico-deductive females, the ones who catch fire on contact with the real and whose sterilized ashes trace strange arabesques in the sky, especially at dusk . . .

A woman may be so heavily made up that you can never be certain of her disappearance. Life can be so mystified that you can never be sure of its opposite.

Never resist a sentence you like, in which language takes its own pleasure and in which, after having abused it for so long, you are stupefied by its innocence. Suddenly, giving pleasure to language is like giving pleasure to a woman – as unexpected, as unconventional, as rare.

Soon spectacles will no longer be a prosthesis but the hereditary attribute of a species which no longer possesses the faculty of sight.

Deep down, no one really believes they have a right to live. But this death sentence generally stays cosily tucked away, hidden beneath the difficulty of living. If that difficulty is removed from time to time, death is suddenly there, unintelligibly.

A particular familiar object has been around for twenty-five years. How many centuries will it be before it disappears? *I* have changed. This just isn't normal. Objects should at least take their share of the responsibilities. That is all I have against the inanimate world.

Imagine a world of mobile, sexed objects, surrounded by a human world that was unsexed and immobile. Objects would have a name, humans would not. We wouldn't be able to stand it. What makes us think they can? Animals, stones, objects are constantly overturning the human order. And we ourselves are hardly out of hell yet.

The TV: every image is an ephemeral vanishing act. But art is the same. In its countless contemporary forms, its only magic is the magic of disappearance, and the pleasures it gives are bloodless ones.

The Oneiropause, worse than the menopause: the end of mental ovulation.

Language is so inarticulate that they had to invent a double articulation to make it inoffensive.

Neither frivolous nor subtle – serious and bestial.
A new form of intellectual bestiality.

Through looking in the mirror, the subject has become haemophilic: coagulation no longer occurs. Through transcendence, the blood no longer stops flowing, nothing heals over.

Dream femininity: it lives only in the heads and desires of men. Women can get together in their millions, but they will never produce that image which can only come from elsewhere. If women don't accept being dreamt of any more, including in the phantasm of violence, then they will lose even their sexual pleasure and their rights. Man has never claimed to free his mind from the spell of female seduction. It is the terrifying prerogative of the liberated sex to claim the monopoly over its own sex: 'I shall not even live on in your dreams.' Man must continue to decide what is the ideal woman.

On the High Plateaus: a tactile illusion of the sphericity of the earth, caused by the clouds – and their shadows on the ground – gliding by so quickly. As, on very bright nights, though somewhat differently, one feels the sphere of the heavens, aerial or starry, following the curvature of the earth's surface. The fact that our world is a sphere seems to have no direct impact on our way of life, on how we represent it, where we readjust everything into linear terms, but it is certainly not without effect on the curvature of our thoughts. There is even in this sphericality of the earth an ironic response to all human 'planning'. If the infrastructure is curved, that changes everything: you have to think curved to embrace the sphericity of the earth and the sky.

It has to be said that writing is an inhuman and unintelligible activity – one must always do it with a certain disdain, without illusions, and leave it to others to believe in one's own work.

Powdered water: just add water to get water.

Their equal panic – hers at the power of ideas and his at sensual frivolity – meant that they got on wonderfully together for many years.

Certain objects echo each other from one end of a culture to the other, and if there was a connection between the Soviets and electricity under the sign of Revolution, there is another between the Unconscious and the freezer under the sign of Involution. Just as food is frozen, so in the Unconscious a mental glaciation of drives and signs takes place. From time to time phantasms, fragments of drives, sequences of signifiers are taken out, which can in fact be defrosted by the intermediary stage, the subconscious, the equivalent of the refrigerator stage – with the psychoanalyst, the Grand Master of the Cold, carrying out the careful defrosting of delusions and dreams in his consulting room.

Freud thought he was bringing the plague to the USA, but the USA has victoriously resisted the psychoanalytical frost by real deep freezing, by mental and sexual refrigeration. They have countered the black magic of the Unconscious with the white magic of 'doing your own thing', air conditioning, sterilization, mental frigidity and the cold media of information.

Holidays are in no sense an alternative to the congestion and bustle of the cities and work. Quite the contrary. People look to escape into an intensification of the conditions of ordinary life, into a deliberate aggravation of those conditions: further from nature, nearer to artifice, to abstraction, to total pollution, to well above average levels of stress, pressure, concentration and monotony – this is the ideal of popular entertainment. No one is interested in overcoming alienation; the point is to plunge into it to the point of ecstasy. That is what holidays are for. And getting a suntan serves as a supernatural proof of this acceptance of the conditions of normal life.

Copying out these notes is indelicate in every respect, and I fear only bad will come of it. This is a sort of death sentence, a kind of violence, for why should I arrest them in their handwritten flow? If they can only be written out longhand, it is because they are neither a book nor a series of thoughts. They must be a secret text, then, but that too is a senseless idea. I have to give them over to chance, to whatever indeterminate fate may be in store for them, or rather, to the happy chance of being caught with their defences down, without the defence literature provides. But this phobia for the literary annoys me too. The diagnosis is simple: there is strictly no reason to hide a mirror in your drawer.

She does everything. She sings in opera, makes films, even produces them. She swims like a god, is as beautiful as a goddess. She was born in Mexico, has a diaphanous skin, deep blue but lively eyes (which is rare). She looks like a liana or a convulvulus in her tight white lamé dress. She speaks five languages – too much, too much. At its height, perfection becomes like virginity. You have to lose it.

Culture contradicts all genetic capital. It is the touch of magic, the special touch which contradicts biology, heredity, etc. and condenses a whole dynasty into one generation.
What cannot be obtained in a single generation is ease and courage. Mutants are cowards.

What comes out of a conflict like the Falklands is an unequal scale of passions between North and South and a parallel escalation of rage. Rage (it's the same with Israel and the Arab countries) at always seeing the weak imbued with contempt for themselves by a sort of capillary action from the superior race, so frightened are they by the revenge that needs to be taken and so much do they prefer to indulge in all their own suicidal fantasies. In the order of passions (which is the true order of power), the same countries and peoples are eternally doomed to resentment, to the hysteria of impotence in the face of the arrogant efficiency of the Whites' strategies. That is what is unbearable and which would lead me to detest the Southern – and the Islamic – peoples for their feeble-mindedness, their suicidal rhetorics, if I did not already detest even more the little hardline Whites, who are so sure they will always have the upper hand.

It is this inequality in passions, in virtue, in courage (all they have left is their deaths) which means that the oppressed peoples will never actually measure up to their own power – and which leads one, paradoxically, to dream of a universe of true relations of force where crushing defeat would at least be justified in terms of the world order.

OCTOBER   1982

The unemployed girls with eyes of jade

A generation has disappeared or changed direction. A backfire against theoretical radicalism – and one in which socialism has played its part. The symbolic murder of the intellectual class, not at all unlike the symbolic murder of the political class by the silent majorities.

Basically there are the two opposite attitudes: nothing has been achieved, there is nothing to hope for, God is against us; everything has been accomplished, the promises have been fulfilled, God is with us.

Both attitudes produce societies without hope, the one because the hopes are already fulfilled, the other because they are unfulfillable. But it is not hope which gives a society its strength, but the belief it has fully realized itself in the present. Iran and the USA, strangely brought together in that failed commando operation in the desert, are two diametrically opposite examples of achieved societies.

Religion functions as a sanction for the ritual operation of society in Iran and for advanced technology in the States.

In Japan, there are twenty-seven terms for translating 'sign' and none for translating 'social'. Rare are the societies that conceive themselves as such.

Japanese 'society' has no use for social, historical and political ideals – and the same is even truer of Brazil or the Islamic world; or even, no doubt, of American society. In the end, we are but a few rare and exceptional collectivities to have developed that delicate bloom, the social contract.

And today it is already disappearing.

Transsexuality is not seductive, it is simply disturbing.

Mere ambiguity between the sexes has nothing in common with the spiritual thrill of seduction.

There is something physically disturbing about the ambiguity of bodies, but there is a metaphysical charm in the duality of the sexes.

Men escape from female sexual demands into androgyny or transvestism – women hide from male demands in modesty or sorcery.

In Italy, the men are affectionate, but the women never are. You feel they have a harsh revenge to wreak, their sensuality is full of bitterness and they are only happy in their lives when surrounded by broken men, swapping them as they swap their hysterical jealousies.

The Italian law on rape punishes 'inducement' (*indurre*), that is to say all form of forced solicitation, of abduction of . . . what? A glance, a gesture, turning the lights down low – all is rape since all is sign. The slightest gesture is a premiss of abduction.* The same is true of the feminist imaginary, which sees no difference between rape and seduction, every advance by the other is an unacceptable infringement of one's space [*une promiscuité inacceptable*].

But what is an inviolable and inalienable body? A dream of castration. The feminist dream is also the dream of the law (habeas corpus).

Not only can there be no seduction, but there can be no rape either without a minimal signal. A being capable of truly extinguishing all signals and emitting no anticipated response would be protected even from violence. This is indeed the attitude we instinctively take when faced with physical aggression or aggressive demands – suppression of the signals of fear or desire.

It is a delicious moment when she comes to bed beside me around five, after dancing the night away. I pretend to be asleep and she knows it. There is an echo of a night of partying in her body, which is now silent next to mine, but the music still rings out in it. Hot meets cold between the sheets: her tired body, overstimulated by light and movement, and mine, dark and motionless, attracting her in its coolness. This odd juxtaposition is reinforced by a certain jealousy: the one has been dancing, the other sleeping. But the superficial electricity of the one dissipates into the other's dreamy depths. The opposite situation has its beauty too, when I come home and lie down beside her sleeping form. The effervescence of the fun one has had dies away in the other's warmth, in their complicitous silence,

*Behind Baudrillard's *prémisse* lies the echo of its homonym, *prémice*, the beginning or first fruits. [Tr.]

like that of beaches at the end of summer when the sun is still hot and there is no one left to enjoy it.

You can't theorize something as the 'accursed share' [*part maudite*] without yourself being part of that curse.

There is, in any case, something ridiculous about explaining things. But the worst thing is to give meaning to something that hasn't got any. *We are all pretenders.**

Fresh and fragrant nudity in the dark, ultraviolet and tranquil nudity beneath the infrared gaze of the voyeur.

You can only distinguish the sublime from the pleasant by the fact that the memory of it grips your heart.

Her head is so light that she leaves no mark upon the pillow. The bed from which she rises is not unmade, the sheets have hardly moved, they have barely assumed her shape. She is so discreet, so light. It is like Chuang Tzu's knife, whose blade is never blunted. Her body just twitches with a few spasms before she falls asleep, the echo of the spasms of pleasure.

---

*In English in original. [Tr.]

A stone whose energy was not dissipated as heat on contact with the ground would bounce back eternally with undiminished elasticity. Without that friction, without that contact, without that energy loss, we would have perpetual motion.

Might what is unthinkable in the physical world nonetheless be the law of the mental world? Could it not be that a thought which lost none of its energy in being used, or in evaporation or in secondary effects, a thought which could remain free of all consequences, influence, or reference, would bounce back indefinitely and maintain this potential springiness, the sovereignty of moving bodies in empty space?

Victor/Victoria

In the disguising of this woman as a man, it is femininity which multiplies its seduction by ambiguity. This woman is much more beautiful in a dinner jacket and, because she remains a woman, with all the seductiveness of the opposite signs. It is no good seducing men, you also have to seduce *the signs* of the masculine.

It isn't homosexual charm that seduces the gangster, it is the divination of femininity through its metamorphosis, it is the presentiment of that femininity in the play of its disappearance.

This sublime form of ambiguity is properly feminine. The other form, the disguising of the masculine as feminine is merely grotesque.

The ending of the film shows this: there is no way that the masculine can play on the signs of the other to bask in its masculinity. This was Nico's magnificent idea years ago, to play the false cross-dresser. The true cross-dresser is monstrous, the false one marvellous.

The fact is that only the feminine retains a power of revelation – for its part, the masculine is no longer any secret, and that is the sad thing about it.

Femininity belongs to the realm of the secret, the masculine to the realm of the obscene. Which makes repressed femininity unbearable (it can no longer be divined), but femininity displayed is odious (it becomes masculine and takes on the characteristics of the transvestite).

The masculine is not made for ambiguity, it only exists in erection and thus always constitutes a mildly comic spectacle (the feminine in disguise is, rather, ironic).

'How can you live with a woman who is playing at being a man?'

'But you, aren't you a gangster pretending not to be?'

'Where is the real person? Where is the pretend person?'

'We are all pretenders. Don't we all live double lives?'

'Aren't we all caught up in the vaudeville of ambiguity?'

Everything ambiguous is feminine. Everything that is no longer ambiguous is masculine in kind. That is the nature of the real sexual difference, which lies neither in sex nor in biology.

The greater the tendency to integrate man into mechanical and systemic effects, the more you have to swim against the tide, towards the hypothesis of the illogical sovereignty and material intelligence of things. This is not a mystical hypothesis. It is the only *funny* one.

A rule remains no less secret for being stated. A secret can be revealed or hidden from view, it becomes no less secret for that. It is even perfectly visible in its essence, but that visibility does not remove its wholly elusive character.

One of life's primal situations: the game of hide and seek. Oh, the thrill of hiding while the others come looking for you, the delicious terror of being discovered, but what panic when, after a long search, the others abandon you! You mustn't hide too well. You mustn't be too good at the game. The player must never be bigger than the game itself.

It's like making a joke which is so subtle that it goes unnoticed and you are reduced to explaining it.

Can we draw some other lesson from this?

There exists, between people in love, a kind of capital held by each. This is not just a stock of affects or pleasure, but also the possibility of playing double or quits with the share you hold in the other's heart. One of the strategies can be to sacrifice it at just the right moment and be the first to say: 'I'm not playing any more', since you then collect all the stakes.

Only therapy makes madness obscene, just as it is the care given to them which makes the handicapped obscene (*handicapped is beautiful*).* It is what drowns the cruelty of evil in the sentimentality of the gaze that is obscene. What is supremely obscene is pity, indecent condescension.

One day at Nanterre, in a course on seduction regularly attended by a speech-impaired and motor-handicapped student who nonetheless insists on speaking all the time – and precisely about seduction – sending a chill shudder through the audience with each of his failed contributions, along comes a beautiful feminist, here to combat seduction as sexist ideology. She sits by the handicapped man and throughout his contribution to the discussion leans tenderly towards him to slip a lighted cigarette into his mouth and make him smoke. Just as if she were sucking him off, she makes this wreck of a man suck on his butt like a mother giving him the breast, using him as both candlestick and alibi, all the while vituperating against males who have nothing in their heads but thoughts of seduction. Beautiful, provocative girl, quietly cooking up her revenge through the poor

*In English in original. [Tr.]

impotent, polio victim, who is himself glowing painfully with pleasure at this unexpected rape. Yes, the roles should have been reversed, but which way? She was making me fume too by the malicious pleasure she was taking in this performance and which I also detected in the contained joy of the pallid, perverse disabled man who had hated me from the start and from whom I had never been able to hide the horror he aroused in me – but what he aroused in me now was much worse, for I identified myself with him under the girl's symbolic caresses. She was enticing me by virtually masturbating him under my very eyes; she was saying to me: 'Look, if you were a mongol or impotent, you would be entitled to my favours, I am raping you through him and you are powerless to stop me.' (Later, when I met her by chance at a party, she started to flirt with me un-scrupulously – but I would rather have been that handicapped student, for the space of a seminar, when she put the cigarette between his lips.)

She did not know him from Adam. It was a stroke of genius to place herself next to him and use him as a foil. It was odious, but it had a touch of genius. But for him, she would merely have been a ridiculous feminist.

I love this clearcut, cruel way of settling accounts, as I love those shafts of wit which mean that the end of the story never gets told. I love that woman shame-fully exploiting a handicapped man to promote her shitty feminism, as I love this other woman who, in response to a compliment about her eyes, offers her lover the gift of one of them.

Where does the stereo effect begin, the point where the hi-fi becomes so uselessly sophisticated that the music is lost in the obsession for its fidelity? Where is the point where the social becomes so uselessly sophisticated that it itself goes into stereo and loses itself in the obsession for security? Today, the obsession with this technicity, this veracity, takes us away from music completely. It creates a false destiny for music as it creates a false destiny for the social – to see its fulfil-ment simply as a matter of perfect execution.

We shall one day have dreams in walkman or video form, dreams to which we can add sound effects, which we can slow down or speed up, like television pictures, or play over a second time if we like them. Perhaps we'll even be able to tune in to other people's dreams on FM and converse by cable in our dreams? Dreams would at last have become a means of communication.

Conversely, the music of the walkman penetrates your body like a dream. Neither inside nor outside, it passes behind your eyes like a cenesthesic tape. But we manipulate it. We no longer accept images or sensations unless we can manipulate them. We don't have any great expectations of the substance of images any more, but we expect everything of their tactile and digital manipulation.

One thing protects us from change: exile. In unreality or at the other end of the world, in melancholy or the South, exile is a marvellous and comfortable structure.

Only the exiled have a land. I know some people who are only close to their country when they are 10,000 kilometres away, driven out by their own brothers. The others are nomads chasing their shadows in the deserts of culture.

There are two sorts of silence. The silence of words and the silence of the voice. This latter touches us more deeply.

John grows up normally, but doesn't talk, and this drives his parents to distraction. When he is about 16, at last, one teatime, he says: 'I'd like a little sugar.' His mother is staggered and asks, 'But John, why have you never said anything up to now?' 'Up to now, everything was perfect.'

If everything is perfect, language is useless. This is true for animals. If animals don't speak, it's because everything's perfect for them. If one day they start to speak, it will be because the world has lost a certain sort of perfection.

'I desire you' is obscene.

'You make me feel very good' is more subtle – the other is here the subject of pleasure, not the object of desire.

Desire wants only orgasm; pleasure seeks to please.

There can't be any desire to please – 'pleasing' is implacable.

In days gone by, pleasing occupied the place of desire – today, desire discharges us from the need to please.

Even age may function as a 'natural' perversion. Women are not so much in search of their fathers as of the simple mystery of another generation, closer to death, but also to a previous life.

B.B.

– My understudy has had an operation for appendicitis.

– You're not going to sleep with the whole world. That's impossible, it's rape.

– I have a real understanding for wild animals who are hunted, by camera lenses, by machine-guns.

– A white Rolls and a black chauffeur.

Woman to the power of woman.

Coming home from a long journey.

How do human beings manage to exist so far from one another and to go about their business with such indifference? How do they manage to pretend to be so timeless in your absence? Amazement at the collusive banality of their lives so many thousands of miles apart, while your experience is of distances reduced to nothing by the surrealistic effect of speed. Amazement at the simultaneity of cities linked by jet in a single diagonal drawn across the night.

In fact, the cities of the world are concentric, isomorphic, synchronic. Only one exists and you are always in the same one. It's the effect of their permanent revolution, their intense circulation, their instantaneous magnetism – so different from the rural universe where a sense of the global simultaneity of exchanges does not exist. Through the short-circuit of the time difference, catching cities red-handed in the act of existing.

The only strategy is to be totally indifferent to either of the two opposing solutions. It is at this point that everything comes effortlessly to you since you don't know what fate you're precipitating yourself into. It's as if ideas appeared from both directions at the same time, since you are equally open to the other's strategy. And if he is defeated, it won't have been by the relation of forces, but because you could just as easily have taken his side. This suggests stratagems and solutions to you before which he can only yield.

If parapsychological or extraterrestrial phenomena were genuine, or even merely plausible, one ought to devote oneself to them entirely, wasting not a single moment. I cannot understand how one could waste even a second on other matters. But this also holds for science. If science is what it is, and truth is what it claims to be, they are worthy of a radical passion. Now, nothing like this actually happens. Not only the masses, but scientists themselves only devote themselves to it half-heartedly. We only feel a relative passion, a casual commitment for truth, the same as we feel for irrational phenomena. Only the *suspense* of science can rouse a sudden interest, but that is the passion for suspense. It is aroused today by the fact that even scientists acknowledge there are no final answers in science.

Today the minute researches of science no longer produce anything but an artificial stereophony, stereonomic and holographic effects (the DNA double helix is one of these), and this mere shadow-play is all one needs to manipulate appearances. But the real that is caught in that way is eversive, if not indeed reversible. Under the subtle torture of science, all it ever confesses is its nonexistence.

The more profound things become, the more they slip away, as they do in a concave mirror. The escape into transcendence, the assumption of the world into some upper realm (the Law, the Idea, God, the Truth) has been replaced by a process of evanescence toward the lower reaches, the narrow escape into immanence.

Where the feminine resuscitates, without ideology, and without sexual hysteria either, in a joyous provocation, in a lascivious form of gratuitous self-exhibition, of ironic scenography of a sex without desire. Light, transparent perversion. New allegory of the body.

Indifferent little further researches
Historical little illuminations
Lascivious little intentions
Artificial little fiddles

Very matutinal little crystal
Very sensual little grey sky
Very private little random possibilities

We the living are never naked. Our gazes, our voices are themselves an
adornment. Only in shame do we stand naked, when language is found wanting.
And in death, of course, which is the worst of offences. But the dead themselves
never left naked for the big sleep. And a woman never sleeps naked either – she
always has a jewel or some makeup, a cream or a thought to serve her as protection against the abyss of sleep.

Electrolyzing gazes.
Feminizing lips.
Androgynizing eyes.
Vaporizing dreams.

The indifference of trees to the historical moment. The indifference of dreams
to interpretation. The indifference of the people to its own triumph. The indifference of the body to the revolution. The dazzling metaphysical spectacle of the
sameness of faces the morning after the revolution. Their features haven't
changed. You expect a violent illumination and yet it's just like sleeping with your
sister. It doesn't change your life.

There is an equal violence in taking the defence of the victims of violence, for
commiseration is obscene.
Physical violence does not wound its victim in his sovereignty. Pity or

solidarity strike him precisely there, in his pride, in what is inhuman in man, what is cruel and haughty in him towards himself.

Cruelty has as its target man capable of being more than he is; pity has as its target man guilty of being just as he is.

If solidarity merely means sharing a wretched fate, as it does most of the time these days, then it is itself nothing but a form of abjection.

To devour someone with your eyes, to break through the cloudcover of their eyelashes, to violate these eyes streaming with tears, till you reach the hypocritical sun lit up by the idea of seduction, to enjoy others through their tears: this is a modern cannibalism of the emotions.

The tangled web of hatreds, of complicities, of rivalries between different schools of thought and of changes in mood causes each atom in the intellectual world, which lives in a state of overexposure to itself and its own bad conscience, to prefer itself, while all the atoms detest each other. There is in all this an unfathomable animosity, a thousand poisonous snakes entangled in communicating vessels. This microsociety has a mutual laceration as its adornment and the initiatory ordeal demanded at the entry to the intellectual sanctuary is this bond of hatred and exclusiveness. This is all a provincial passion, exacerbated by the sophistication of the means of expression available. The fact that certain disconcerting effects of beauty and truth may spring forth from time to time from this dungheap of human relations remains a miraculous paradox to be counted among the oddities of existence or ascribed to the ruses of virtue.

It is a long time now since the credits started going further than the films themselves in audacity, humour and the elliptical art of handling images. And if the difference is not so great as it was, that's because the films themselves have taken a lead from the credits.

Behind the pile of information, we can hardly see what is going on in the firmament of current affairs. But what is happening in the firmament of the not-so-current? There is no critical distance any more, there is only pure distance. And this is not engendered by any objection to means or ends, but by an effect of the destruction of causes. Pure distance results from a withdrawal of the object into radical objectivity. New passions are emerging, and those which shine out brightest are humour, objective chance, astronomical complexity, fascination, allegory, ellipsis, indifference and impatience.

The work of the negative. Having ended in history, this has also come to an end in the video or digital image: no more negative, no more depth, less definition (only close-ups work well). Immediate positive synthesis of the image. Tactile and digital: the image no longer made present by the sense of sight, but by the digital sense, which is a sense designed for processing and control.

Vélizy. All those shepherds in the Pyrenees who are being fitted out with fibre optics, radio relay stations and cable TV. Obviously the stakes are pretty high! And not just in social terms. Did these people think they were already living in society, with their neighbours, their animals, their stories? What a scandalously underdeveloped condition they were in, what a monstrous deprivation of all the blessings of information, what barbaric solitude they were kept in, with no possibility of expressing themselves, or anything.

We used to leave them in peace. If they were called on, it was to get them to come and die in the towns, in the factories or in a war. Why have we suddenly developed a need for them, when they have no need of anything? What do we want them to serve as witnesses of? Because we'll force them to if we have to: the new terror has arrived, not the terror of 1984, but that of the twenty-first century. The new negritude has arrived, the new servitude. There is already a roll-call of the martyrs of information. The Bretons whose TV pictures are restored as soon as possible after the relay stations have been blown up . . . Vélizy . . . in the Pyrenees. The new guinea pigs. The new hostages. Crucified on the altar of information, pilloried at their consoles. Buried alive under information. All this to make them admit the inexpressible service that is being done to them, to extort from them a confession of their sociality, of their 'normal' condition as associated anthropoids.

Socialism is destroying the position of the intellectual.

Unlearn what they say. Either they don't believe in it themselves or the violent effort they make to believe in it is disagreeable.

We are in a period in which the mental and intellectual structures are burying themselves, becoming interred in memories, archives, far from the sun, in search of silent efficiency or an improbable resurrection. All thoughts are burying themselves in prudent preparation for the Year 2000. They can already sense the coming terror of the Year 2000. They are instinctively adopting the solution of those cryogenized individuals who are immersed in liquid nitrogen until a technique can be found to ensure their survival. They are like those funereal commodities locked away in the underground sarcophagus of the *Forum des Halles* as a potential museum, an excavation site for the post-catastrophe generations. They

night air of the Côte des Neiges. Neither Latin sensuality, nor American dis-embodiment, but an ironic liberty that is the product of a winter civilization, a hyperboreal form of tenderness and sexual insolence, a new form of femininity perhaps . . .

There is more to fashion than a sociology of distinction can express. It is a collective passion. Culture in general is more than a differential mechanism, it is the form of prestige which a whole society without distinction confers upon itself, by an impassioned concatenation of forms, of language, of signs, which is a challenge to the grammatical order of differences, though at the same time rooted within it. It seems we have lost this demiurgic version of culture and lapsed into the semio- and sociological version.

You are consumed by passion, but [in French] you feed on obsessions. Obsession is the alimentary form of passion.

When a woman is naked, the weather clouds over
When the weather clouds over, her eyes are clear
When her eyes cloud over, her belly is warm

We are in shifting circumstances in which nothing is hidden and everything is mobile – a world of a quite new kind of innocence, but a world no longer illuminated by the utopian constellation of secrecy.
The individual is less alienated by the fact that everything is known about him than by the fact that he is called upon to know everything about himself. In this demand lies the principle of a new and irreversible servitude.

There is much more to be hoped for in an excess of information or of weapons than in the restriction of information or arms control.

*Da, wo die Gefahr wächst, wächst das Rettende auch.**

In Quebec, during a strike, the students occupied the computer room. Not because they wanted to knock out a nerve centre of imperialism, but simply because it was winter and it was the only place where they could keep warm, since the authorities could not run the risk of turning off the current, for fear of corrupting the computer memories.

Beauty is not negotiable since its radiance simply emerges irrespective of any efforts made to deserve it, and no one can offer it its equivalent. Its annihilation it must also perform *itself*. That was what drugs were to her: a calculated abjection, a denial of her own radiant beauty, suicide.

You only need to talk about one woman to another to awaken in the one the idea of replacing the other. A woman only has to talk to you about another woman for you to want to transfer your affections from her to the other. It is madness to deny the existence of this transferential infidelity.

If it were confronted with its ideological objectives and its stated aims, Soviet society would immediately collapse. But – and the reason for this is both a disappointment and a mystery – it remains intact. You can easily forget that it

*'But where there is danger, there grows/Also what saves.' (Hölderlin). In German in original. [Tr.]

does so only on account of a collective collusion in the *comedy* of ideology, the *comedy* of bureaucracy. As a general rule, any society only continues to exist by collusion in the *deriding* of its own model.

This truth is also strikingly evident in Italy. In this case, however, the situation is reversed, for there the state is weak, its institutions in confusion and its principles corrupted. This is, however, immaterial, because derision recreates a mysterious social consensus and a cunning solidarity which prevents the whole system from collapsing.

Peep-show, striptease:* the indifference of the body to the gaze directed at it. Bodies tactile in their presence, and yet intact in their essence, when their undulations forbid the onlooker's gaze to rest on them. Invulnerable transcendence of woman and her body. Bodies haloed by their sexual attributes which are like the finery of some animal – what sex is deep down and why we marvel at it. It is, therefore, a wholly spiritual passion for theatrical production which guides this spectacle, as it guided nature in the magnificent staging of the species and their differences.

Idle, archaic, indifferent mentality. I am beginning to feel I might give all this up, as if the challenge were not worth the trouble, might give up all judgement. This state of mind has been with me from childhood, from adolescence – a lacklustre, slipshod, idle, irresponsible, uncultivated, undesiring state.

These books, did they ever interest me? These women, did I ever feel any emotion for them? All these different countries, did I want to discover them?

Only the inhumanity of things has affected me, and I have in fact been

---

*In English in original. [Tr.]

unable to bring this into my own life. I read this verdict in the graph of the tonality of events, of the melancholy of faces, of the vanity and futility of our undertakings. I am still astonished by the mirror we can offer to others, by the loving or ironic image which we still are sometimes in each others' mirrors.

Increasingly, it is machines, not people, who get nervous. People only become nervous if they force themselves to look like machines.

All situations where you have to make a choice come down to this: do you prefer a woman with a very ordinary body but an attractive face, or one whose body is attractive, but whose face is nothing special? The problem is a false one. It is always preferable to be in a situation where there is no choice to be made either because the woman is perfect, or because she is the only one available.

The Dream: a heavy lorry carrying a block of hewn marble collides with the columns of a building which looks like Versailles or St Peter's, Rome. The lorry overturns and the driver gets out, cursing. In the meantime, the whole façade of the building sways and slowly collapses. And, at that point, like rats leaving a sinking ship, all the statues, which up till then had remained motionless in their various positions, upright, stooping, or leaning back, slowly begin to wake, to stir, to open their eyes and run off to escape the disaster. Were they human beings who had been playing this role for centuries? They had been waiting for the end to break free.

This extraordinary capacity of women for survival (even in love and breakup) which comes easy to them, since, after all, they were on the scene nine months before you, and so will be there nine months after you too. Measured time begins at birth; but the other kind of time began before that. Woman, who holds sway over this antenatal time, is logically also in control of time after death.

Dallas. The scriptwriters have each of the actresses in the soap opera play the death scene in the swimming pool: they do not know which of them is to die, and hence disappear from the series.

The 'soap' becomes their destiny. If they should die in reality, a way is devised for writing them out of the script. If they are sacrificed in the script, their stardom inevitably comes to an end in real life too, since they are identified with the characters they play.

It is the same as in a ceremony: outside the ritual, you count for nothing, but the ritual is flexible enough to make use of all the chance happenings of life. *Dallas*'s secret lies in its closeness to tribal and initiatory stereotypes. That is why there is never any laughter in it: no wit, no humour, no comic episodes, no happy coincidences. It is a closed world in which everything leads inevitably to fatality, perfidy, sentimental incest or magical cannibalism. Such is the tribal law, of which J.R. is the emblem, which gives rise to the desperate efforts on the part of the women to escape from this archaic trap.

In its artless cruelty, *Dallas* is superior to any 'intelligent' critique that can be made of it. That is why intellectual snobbery meets its match here.

In a dream I saw the face of servitude. It is the face of a woman with heavy-lidded, blue, expressionless eyes. The crescent shapes of her breasts are asymmetrical. She always has a smile for the poorest as she crawls off daintily towards infinity.

Boredom is like a pitiless zooming in on the epidermis of time. Every instant is dilated and magnified like the pores of the face.

Luxury in trains or planes today consists in being spoken to. You are kept in a state of information about the journey, a state of alert about your own body (a good metabolism, relax) of cultural stimulation (music, films), and even in a subliminal question-and-answer state (the tactile language of the woman announcer, the air hostess's 'voiceover'). Whether you are travelling at 180 m.p.h. or in the sky at 600 m.p.h., you do not leave the semiosphere. That's the luxury of 'business class'.

Everyone else is carted around like cattle.

The mystic dream of every iceberg is to travel as far south as possible, perhaps – who knows? – till it meets its end in equatorial waters. Poor iceberg laden with the despair of the poles at being so far from the equator, and so distant from each other. So far, not a single one of them has succeeded in this senseless venture.

Dying away like the wind at the day's end
Ending like an idol lit up on all sides
Smiling at this diffuse light which envelops the objects of denial
Saluting the point of no return
Zarathustra. Twilight ethics

The scandal of the end of the world will not occur, for the very good reason that existence has already been judged and declared unjustifiable. This world must thus be considered the only one there'll ever be, the verdict immanent, injustice irremediable. This has nothing to do with the natural tendency of things but rather with the bestial ethic smouldering in the labyrinthine entrails of human beings, which requires that the just be separated from the unjust, the good from the bad, so that the truest, stupidest and most sentimental order may triumph.

In fact there is no need to wait. Let the stupidest things triumph, that is the Last Judgement.

When you have lumbago, you have to move like a reptile. You have to get through your movement before the muscle has had time to feel pain. It is the same with ideas and language. You have to have got to the end of the sentence, before language has had time to feel pain.

The omega point of a system is the point of a pure circulation of energies destined, by the very fact of that circulation, to indifference and death. In such a system exchange becomes impossible owing to an immanent equivalence – every particle is in suspense before the only possible event: the meeting with the antiparticle which will cancel it out. It is at this point that the entire system nears the alpha point of another mechanism. Beyond a certain phase the whole system tends towards this fatal point.

Radical objectivity is the exact opposite of the objectivity of science. The one addresses the rationality of partial processes, the other the irony of the overall process.

Women constitute a secret society. They are all involved together in secret discussions. Those I have known – none of whom have known the others except by accident – nonetheless weave amongst themselves a collusive web of seduction. They signal to each other, as the events in a lifetime signal to each other in their apparently indifferent spiral. Moreover, each one, with an unacknowledged fervour, envelops all her rivals, past and future, in the same field of jealousy, fascination and complicity – and in turn she is all the others together, those whom you have kept apart in life, finally united in the only real secret society – the dream society, the society of women.

Reversibility, like that of day and night, of all the concepts at the equatorial heart of the system: this paradoxical, derisory, indefensible and therefore impregnable position is the bitter privilege of phantom rhetorics.

As for freedom, it will soon cease to exist in any shape or form. Living will depend upon absolute obedience to a strict set of arrangements, which it will no longer be possible to transgress. The air traveller is not free. In the future, life's passengers will be even less so: they will travel through their lives fastened to their (corporate) seats.

Theory must not only be cut off from its reference, but also from any commentary: it's not normal to carry out an autopsy on a newborn child.

Is not the world itself, once it is removed from the nightmare of objectivity perpetrated by science – the intention of which was to pay it impartial homage – an effect without a cause? And thus also without consequence. There is no sense, then, in musing on its failure.

All these poor old people, these guinea-pigs of retirement who, freed at last from sex and work, hoped to find rest in a sort of indifference to life and an anticipated pleasure of death, by far the best way of growing old – no one will be able to say we have left them a place in the sun at the end of the road. No, they have to be persecuted to the bitter end, retrained, libidinalized (have fun! get into something! it's never too late), culturalized (theatre, cinema, discussion groups, yoga, sixteenth-century music) – no efforts will be spared to enable them to die stupid.

Gradual cessation of activity, visual handicap, impairment of speech and hearing, etc.: all euphemisms. Words themselves have fallen victim to a shameful illness. A cat is no longer a cat, it is an associated feline. Language is defenceless.

There was, in Aztec thinking, the idea that the sun only shines to fulfil a symbolic obligation, and that men must know how to pay the price for this. This is the universe of cruelty. We, by contrast, believe the *function* of the sun is to shine for everyone by virtue of the rights of man and equality of opportunity. A sorry challenge which the sun rejects. We seem to have been having far less sunshine of late.

Language can no longer allow itself to be caught up with the philosophical theatricality of its object. It must also itself become an attack by fascination.

Instead of making a note of a particular appointment at a certain time, I note down the time alongside the time. Next to Tuesday evening, I write 'Tuesday evening' – completely unable to make this juxtaposition coincide with any point in time. It's rather like the sign which is signalling to itself and orders you not to see it. *'Ignore this sign.'**

The way the bumble-bee holds itself motionless in mid-air, its energy derived from the fact that it makes no sound. The flowers are moved by this silent conjugality.

Silent little dirty tricks
Felonious little anomalies
Interstitial little offences
Pulpy little transgressions
The medusas of the exception
are the solution petrified
by the ruse of broken lines.

Beaubourg: the sacred rubbish-heap of stockpiled values (the fifth floor) – the desacralized rubbish-heap of free expression (the piazza). Added to which today is a heap of real rubbish caused by a strike among the maintenance staff. A logical strike this, since its demand is that the management of refuse disposal be included in culture (there is at this very moment an exhibition of refuse at Beaubourg) and that the staff should be directly employed by the institution. Yet the latter, for all its devotion to mobility, versatility and the absorption of the heteroclite, seems incapable of mastering this situation. It will die, therefore, of its own waste, and in so doing serve as a model to postmodern civilization. Beaubourg is destined to

*In English in original. [Tr.]

exercise the fascination of dead centres, to suffer pestilence and pillage. It is an object that is wrecked before it even begins, a monument to continual absorption and evacuation, an involutive, voracious, fractal zone, where parasitisms are pushed to the limit and lines of demarcation vanish, giving way simply to the incestuous virulence of the multitude fallen prey to itself. Let us leave it this spectral quality of putrid object, condemned to rapid degradation – the only modern object we have produced, unintentionally.

What sense would there be in blending in these urban monsters (Beaubourg, La Villette, La Défense, Opéra, Bastille, etc.) with the city or the surrounding area? They are not monuments; they are monsters. They testify not to the integrity of the city but to its disintegration, not to its organic nature but to its disorganization. They do not provide a rhythm for the city and its exchanges; they are projected on to it like extraterrestrial objects, like spacecraft falling to earth from some dark catastrophe. Neither centre nor periphery, they mark out a false centrality and around them lies a false sphere of influence; in reality they reflect the satellization of urban existence. Their attraction serves only to impress the tourists, and their function, like that of airports and places of interchange in general, is that of a place of expulsion, extradition, and urban ecstasy. Moreover, this is what all the alternative groups and the subculture that congregate there are primarily looking for: an empty ecstasy, an icefloe in outer space, a cosmopolitan strand, a parasitic site . . . We must take them as they are – monsters they are; monsters we must leave them.

Blindly: that is the only elegant way to love. What reproach could there be for someone who discreetly and totally devotes himself to another; what reproach could there be for someone who is the object of such devotion? Blind destination: that is the direction dreams go, in ideas and love.

All this soft, rich little world wakes up every morning reflected off its gardens and the nearby sea. Fine, lean horses graze between the tulip fields and heavy girls with bright eyes pedal furiously around the streets of Amsterdam. Despite the obvious signs of *savoir-vivre*, including alternative social and sexual forms, history has left no trace here of a genuine culture or, in other words, of a charm, a distinction, a superfluity, a stylized violence, as it has in Italy.

They seem to carry in their bodies these long diphthongs, the vowels of a dialect language, *niederdeutsch* which seems not to have achieved the agility and decantation of true language. These bourgeois folk have cultivated a provincial worldwideness which is fat, solid and guttural. There is a hazy, dappled sky over Roosendaal. When, oh when was this land at the centre of the world, with Spinoza's ravings about substance and Vermeer's light?

In this town where everyone kept running into everyone else, whom they knew, I just kept running into my own face and name on the walls.

And I placed my fingers on her eyes as though I were touching the silent controls of a TV set. Those places which one only touches lightly – the eyes of course, certain soft parts of the body, impervious to sexuality, which wish neither to be penetrated nor violently caressed – where the blood courses lightly beneath the surface of the skin, where meaning courses lightly beneath the surface of words.

The ferocity of women towards one another. No sooner has one 'got' her man, than not only does she look pityingly upon the other, but sees to it that she feels all her misery too.

mutant in the motor and sensory domain. It is no accident that the social is increasingly being organized around him: the blind person and the spastic constitute testing grounds, interesting mechanisms which it seems proper to cerebralize, whilst at the same time socializing them for form's sake. They have it in them to become wonderful instruments, precisely because they are immobilized and therefore marked down for automatism and remote control. The normal man will never make such a good automaton as someone who is disabled or spastic. There is nothing new in all this. It was eunuchs who provided the most beautiful voices in the choirs of the Renaissance.

In summer you hear dogs howling in the evening, you see insomniacs tending their plants in the middle of the night, you can read in lifeless, blazing eyes that anguished euphoria characteristic of the longer days, of the relentless sun, of that extraversion of heat which forces you into a pure and objectless physical pleasure and which for many amounts to a situation verging upon suicide. Those who stay in the towns seem to be walking a tightrope. They know that while the others are away they are keeping sociality going. In much the same way as they water the neighbour's geraniums while he is away – yet both groups are taking on a historic and dramatic role: the one that of abandoning the city for who knows what exodus of pleasure, the other that of keeping an eye on the set. In fact, it is a wholesale catastrophe. The town is playing out its exodus, it is emptying without having been bombed; it is delivering itself up to its slaves (the immigrants) in a fleeting Saturnalia.

Several girls, naked and virginal, are playing around in a bathtub. I ask them what they are playing at. They say they are playing the social elephants game.

Temperatures, petrol prices, the price of the dollar: the golden triangle of our summer. These are facts beyond our control and all we hope now is to see them all rising indefinitely. Sometimes the figures are mixed up in a prophetic confusion, as in 1980 in the US deserts. There, the price per gallon: $1.18, $1.20, $1.25, varied from one place to another as an exact reflection of the temperature graphs: 100, 110 and 120 degrees Fahrenheit. With the question of confidence always lurking just beneath the surface: what price would you accept petrol rising to? What point do you think the dollar could go up to (with the implication: before causing a crash in world economies)? What record level can the heat reach (before causing a volatilization of energy and the beginnings of a worldwide insomnia)? Our artificial destiny is written in these asymptotic curves.

The social year stops when summer starts. For eight months of the year, the cold, the social, democracy and political necessities prevail. When summer arrives, another atmosphere takes over: the heat, terrorism, accidents, olympic records, the 'silly season', folk culture and the silence of the intellectuals. It is the same each year. Even the return from the holidays isn't what it used to be. There are no more great social tides at the equinoxes. Only a pendular movement from one solstice to another.

The immorality of those families whose children are burnt alive on motorways. They have money heaped on them by social welfare institutions and they go and spend it on consumer goods, which the right-thinking regard as sordid. But they have never had to see their kids die before they could buy a car and, hence, have never felt the need to send them off for inexpensive holidays on those coaches which, as if by chance, always have fatal accidents.

The immorality of those who eat their children in hard cash merely corresponds to the immorality of the social institution which recompenses their death.

Everything in this vicious circle is abject: chance, which kills the poorest children, social charity which turns their deaths into a source of income, the parents who benefit from it to enjoy a short spell of wealth and decent society which stigmatizes them, for rumour does not condemn them at all for their indiscreet behaviour but for not handling the money rationally by putting it in the bank, for example, but instead spending it unscrupulously, thus verifying that they were indeed the victims of a divine justice.

The whole of the social is there in its logical abjection. It is the poor who die and it is they who deserved to. It is this mediocre truth, this mediocre fatality which we know as 'the social'.

Which amounts to saying that it only exists for its victims. Wretched in its essence, it only affects the wretched. It is itself a disinherited concept and it can only serve to render destitution complete. Nietzsche is right: the social is a concept, a value made by slaves for their own use, beneath the scornful gaze of their masters who have never believed in it.

This can be clearly seen in all the so-called social reforms which inescapably turn against the intended beneficiaries. The reforms strike those whom they should save. This is not a perverse effect. Nature herself conforms to this willingly and catastrophes have a preference for the poor. Has a catastrophe ever been seen which directly strikes the rich – apart perhaps from the burial of Pompeii and the sinking of the *Titanic*?

Male eroticism in advertising is always ridiculous. Those who argue for it as the equivalent of the 'erotic prostitution' of the female body on the public stage have no understanding of the mental play of images. The success of the erotic hallucination of the feminine (even for women) comes from the translucidity of those arses, their perfection as objects of idolatry. Only the feminine lends itself to this hallucination. The masculine is never transparent, it cannot be hallucinated. Once it appears, with its ponderousness, its affectation, the magic of the object is gone. The masculine performs poorly on the stage of illusion: whatever thinks it is a subject is always exposed to ridicule by the play of appearances.

All it can do is disappear.

If we consider the superiority of the human species, the size of its brain, its powers of thinking, language and organization, we can say this: were there the slightest possibility that another rival or superior species might appear, on earth or elsewhere, man would use every means at his disposal to destroy it. Humans won't tolerate any other species – not even a superhuman one: they see themselves as the climax and culmination of the earthly entreprise, and they keep a vigorous check on any new intrusion in the cosmological process. Now there is no reason why this process should come to a halt with the human species, but, by universalizing itself (though only over a few thousand years) that species has more or less fixed it that an end be put to the occurrence of the world, assuming for itself all the possibilities of further evolution, reserving for itself a monopoly of natural and artificial species.

This is not the ferocity of wild and predatory animal species, for these are part of cycles, and are located within constantly reversible hierarchies: neither their appearance nor their disappearance ever puts an end to the process. Only man invents a hierarchy against which there is no possible appeal, in which he is the keystone. This is a sort of ferocity raised to the second power, a disastrous pretension.

The ferocity of man as a species is reflected in the ferocity of humanism as a way of thinking: his claim to universal transcendence and his intolerance of other types of thought is the very model of a superior racism.

Whilst they are hardly to be seen in real life these days, the most intense passions continue to figure in our dreams. Are these then a reserve of fresh and timeless energy, running beneath the stages of life (and perhaps reaching beyond the mishap that is death)? Or is this freshness not merely the hallucination of a jaded desire? In other words: are there two lines to our lives, the one of a non-biological, immemorial youth, which we experience in dreams, and the other an organic line of life and death, of duration and of remembrance, with which we identify our pale and mortal existence? Could there be two fundamental sequences and no relation between them? Or is the first simply the projection of the second, its hallucinatory discourse, as, deep down, psychoanalysis argues?

I am for the first hypothesis: we have two existences, each of which is wholly original and independent of the other (it is not a case of a psychological splitting). Neither existence can be used to interpret the other – which is why psychoanalysis is futile.

There is certainly some interplay between body and mind. The weaker the body, the more apparent the organic wretchedness or obsolescence of that machine, the freer and the more adventurous one's thinking becomes. It too partakes of that sort of timeless youth which has nothing whatever to do with being in the prime of life. Thinking lives on neither health nor vitality, but on lucidity and pride, and the decaying of the body stimulates that lucidity and that pride.

There is nothing worse than this obligation to research, to seek out references and documentation that has taken up residence in the realm of thought and which is the mental and obsessional equivalent of hygiene. In the 'intellectual field', as it is so aptly called, one has to plough the furrow of the concept. It is true that we no longer have a culture of leisure, in which thought and writing were violent and pleasurable. And our leisure now is no more than the charnel-house where dead time is born.

The anxiety specific to leisure and the Coast. Too many forms of natural beauty artificially brought together. Too many villas, too many flowers. Villegiatura, nomenklatura: the same struggle. The same artificial privilege, whether it be that of the political bureaucracy or the luxuriance of lifestyle. Nature putrefied by leisure, purged of all barbarity, sickeningly comfortable – one day perhaps this dream climate, this heatwave of luxury will explode into one last forest fire.

The book must break up so as to resemble the ever increasing number of extreme situations. It must break up to resemble the flashes of holograms. It must roll around on itself like the snake on the mountains of the heavens. It must turn all the figures of style on their head. It must fade away as it is being read. It must laugh in its sleep. It must turn in its grave.

If there is a species which is more maltreated than children, then it must be their toys, which they handle in an incredibly off-hand manner (how long will it be before someone starts a society for the protection of battered and maltreated objects?). Toys are thus the end point in that long chain in which all the conditions of despotic high-handedness are in play which enchain beings one to another, from one species to another – from cruel divinities to their sacrificial victims, from masters to slaves, from adults to children, and from children to their objects. This is actually the only strong symbolic chain, the one through which a victim of the whim of a superior power passes it on to an inferior species, the whole process ending with someone taking it out on a powerless simulacrum, like a toy – and beginning no doubt with an all-powerful simulacrum, like the masked divinities which men themselves invent to justify this wretched chain.

The mind's real power (what else can we call it?) is its ability to distinguish a particular nerve, fibre or infinitesimal articulation of the body and invest or disinvest it at will (a sudden thought produces pain in an unknown muscle, or makes a particular line of the face smile, but not some other). The mind can exert itself upon a particular fraction of the body which cannot be located anatomically, as it can on a particular particle of language which cannot be located linguistically, or a particular fraction of time which cannot be located chronologically.

We end up doing everything for reasons of mental hygiene. Thinking out of mental hygiene, to keep in good shape intellectually. Screwing out of mental hygiene, to keep in good shape sexually. Socializing out of mental hygiene to keep in good shape operationally. All our activities are attuned to this hygienic objective. The modern person, condemned to obsolescence like a piece of military hardware, must nonetheless remain in a functioning state. Why? For no reason. For his mental health. Isn't the production system just a vast apparatus that we keep going for the sake of the workers' mental health?

Beautiful as the sensual panorama of discrimination
Beautiful as the sensual illusion of the orifices of the body
Beautiful as the aesthetic division of the work of households
Beautiful as the succession of phases of the light of day

The proximity of bodies in the dark, the tactile promiscuity of objects, the confusion of desires in dreams – these are the fundamental qualities, and they are qualities of the night.

A study of the differential resistance of the skin of the buttocks of the two sexes to blood pressure – there's a fine subject for research in a sterile and functional future.

On the truth of things, three hypotheses:
- That things are as they are makes them true (this is the empirical version).
- That they cannot be other than as they are does not prevent them from being true (though it is not really clear why: this is the confused and paradoxical version).
- That they cannot but be as they are is what prevents them from being true. The necessity of being such takes from them the ring of truth (this is the negative and subtle version).

The seal of secrecy is a fine metaphor. The secret is in fact that which is sealed, that which circulates beneath the seal of appearances and not beneath the sign of communication (not even beneath the opposite sign of the unsaid and silence). The secret is what has no need of being said and is therefore the most obvious of things and shines forth in full daylight, needing no other form of expression.

One way of dying is to make your death alter the state of things in such a way that you no longer have any reason to be a part of it. Thus death can have the effect of a prophetic disappearance. Such were the deaths of Barthes and Lacan, I believe: the world has taken another direction since, in which these subtle figures would no longer have had any meaning. The death of Sartre, by contrast, left the world unchanged and seems an ineluctable, but insignificant event. Before dying, he was already to live in a world that was no longer his own.

So far as existence is concerned, as Ajar* would say, it needs to be taken in charge by someone. No one can be expected to bear the responsibility for their own life. This Christian and modern idea is a vain and arrogant proposition. Moreover, it is a groundless utopian notion. The individual would have to be able to transform himself into the vestal, or the slave, of his identity, control all his circuits and all the circuits of the world which meet in his genes, nerves and thoughts. An unprecedented state of servitude. Who would wish to have salvation at such a price?

It is so much more human to put one's fate, one's desire, one's will into the hands of another. Circulation of responsibilities, declension of wills, perpetual transfer of forms. Apart from this subtle path, which is attested to by a great many cultures, there is only the totalitarian path of a collective assumption.

The old form of voluntary servitude was that of free men using that freedom paradoxically to turn themselves into serfs. The new voluntary servitude is that of men obeying the demand that they be free.

What you look for in travel is neither discovery nor exchange, but a gentle deterritorialization, being taken in charge by the journey itself, and therefore by absence. In the metallic vectors which transcend the meridians, the oceans and the poles, absence takes on a carnal quality. The secrecy of hiding away in one's private life gives way to annihilation by latitude and longitude. But in the end the body wearies of not knowing where it is, whilst the mind is excited by that absence, as if by a lively, subtle quality that is its own. The body is woven of too many ties of blood and flesh. It resists this disfiguring of familiar space in the anamorphosis of travel.

*The novelist Romain Gary's alter-ego. [Tr.]

All things considered, what we look for in other people is perhaps the same gentle deterritorialization we look for in travel. The temptation of exile in the desire of another and of journey across that desire come to be substituted for one's own desire and for discovery. Often looks and amorous gestures already have the distance of exile, language expatriates itself into words which are afraid to mean, the body is like a hologram, gentle on the eyes and soft to the touch, and can thus easily be striated in all directions by desire like an aerial space. We move circumspectly within our emotions, passing from one to another, on a mental planet made up of convolutions. And we bring back the same transparent memories from our excesses and passions as we do from our travels.

The more advanced life-simulation technology becomes, the more the question of the soul intervenes, perversely, as an accident. Everything becomes transformed into a pure, incessant production of accidents. From the moment we leave the world of substance and come to live in that of accident, perversion becomes normal and constitutive.

She disliked the fact that men would always want to take a woman there-and-then, without delay . . . One day, she gets her own back. She does not take the lift, but goes up the stairs instead and undresses floor by floor – her sweater, her skirt, her shoes, her watch, finally, just outside the door, her knickers; then she rings the bell. When I open the door she is standing there completely naked, like a dream, with her raincoat over her arm. The most beautiful present she could give me (but also, what artifice there is in immodesty!).

What she did not say was that she wanted to be undressed slowly with all the ceremonial that should go into unveiling a perfect body, which would only finally be penetrated with extreme politeness, almost out of consideration for the difference between the sexes, a delicate seduction which women dream of as intensely as men dream of the opposite.

Right from the start our relationship had gone astray over this divergence. Sometimes she had imposed her dream of sensual attentiveness. This time, she was giving herself to me – far beyond my own wildest dreams. At least she was pretending to. For, renouncing the game of femininity, she it was once again who was overturning the rules.

They say other species have stopped short, and that only the human species, the humanoid branch, has made its definitive breakthrough. In fact while all the others persevered in their specific forms and ended up disappearing genetically, thus leaving evolution to run its course, only the human species succeeded in surpassing itself in the simulacrum of itself – in disappearing genetically to resuscitate artificially. By perpetuating itself in a world of clones and electronic prostheses (perfect in so far as they will have eliminated every potential species, including humanity), man will thus, in a definitive act, have wiped out the natural genesis of things.

Contact with the men who wield power and authority still leaves an intangible sense of repulsion. It's very like being in close proximity to faecal matter, the faecal embodiment of something unmentionable and you wonder what it is made of and where it acquired its historically sacred character. Why this feeling of loathing for the politician? Is it the impression of being artificially subjected to a will that is even more stupid than your own and which, by its very function, has to be crude? How can the decision-making function be performed without simplifying the mechanisms of thought?

Political charisma is precisely not that gracious charisma which emanates from the irresistible power of a pure object, such as the power of a woman, but an ungracious will which derives its power and its glory from voluntary servitude. This is true of all institutions, the military, the clerical, the medical, and more recently the psychoanalytic, but it is particularly so in politics which remains the most striking hallucination of all the weaknesses of the will.

One may justify the existence of men in power in many different ways. Yet power remains a pernicious thing for what justifies it is inexpiable.

Fragility, which belongs to the realm of appearances, is to be preferred to the fractal which is merely the quality of a mathematical object.

It is exciting to hear one of your fondest ideas formulated in one fell swoop, better than you could have done it yourself. You feel no intellectual jealousy at seeing yourself outstripped in this way. You only feel jealous when you are overtaken by your shadow.

Two bodies side by side, which are not asleep and know it: a strange kind of communication sets in between them, formed of respect for simulated sleep, and yet it needs to betray itself by some furtive sign – a breathing pattern which is not that of real sleep or movements which are not those of a dreaming body. Neither, however, wants to break the spell. It is a conspiracy in the dark, an emotional conspiracy filled with delicious tension.

There has been much discussion of the uninterpretable answer to the question: 'are you lying?' But ask someone next to you, very softly so as not to wake him: 'are you asleep?' If he replies that he is, then that makes him a liar. But he can reply by pretending to be asleep, which is not actually lying, but pretending to lie. There is a big difference, since this is a lovers' game. The question itself is a lovers' game because it assumes the partner is not asleep while making every effort not to wake him. Besides, these are the same questions: do you love me? are you lying to me? are you asleep? And the reply – yes, I love you, yes, I'm lying, yes, I'm asleep – is equally paradoxical. But it is not untruthful. It simply comes from another world which is not the truth of the first. 'Yes, I'm asleep. Yes, I'm lying. Yes, I love you': all these answers reflect a marvellous somnambulism and, all in all, a very clear grasp of the relations we establish with reality when we are sleeping, lying or in love.

O C T O B E R   1 9 8 3

The long lightning flashes of the first flood

The price we pay for the complexity of life is too high. When you think of all the effort you have to put in – telephonic, telepathic, technological and relational – to alter even the slightest bit of behaviour in this strange world we call social life, you are left pining for the straightforwardedness of primitive peoples and their physical work. This is particularly true of unnecessary mental complexities. One should always prefer pure physical effort and, for preference, keep mental energy for sensual pleasures alone.

The sad thing about artificial intelligence is that it lacks artifice and therefore intelligence.

In the early morning and the semiconsciousness of awakening, in this quiet street, which affluence lends a provincial charm even though it is in the very heart of Paris, there is suddenly a solitary sound, which appears to rise up from the depths of your dreams: the shrill clatter of the high heels of a woman whom the daily coming of the light sends scurrying toward her work. The sound begins at the end of the street, grows as she passes beneath the window, in a great hurry, merciless in the morning light (nobody would ever walk like this at night) then dies away towards the other end. She took an eternity to walk the length of this street, though it is not long, so harshly did the indomitable metallic reverberation seem to condemn the noiseless, sleepy world all around. I am sure that the woman was well aware of this, and that it was the only pleasure of her day.

Childish despair: this woman I meet in my dream, fall passionately in love with and give my address to – I immediately realize that the address is wrong and she has no chance of ever finding me, either in the dream or in real life, to which I can already sense I am returning. But why, why did I give her that wrong address? Even after waking, I agonize over this all day.

He gives all sorts of people the impression that he has got exactly what they are looking for. Subtlety for the subtle. Warm-heartedness for the warm-hearted. For the brutal, brutality. For crooks, sharp practice. Atrocity for the atrocious. Whatever you want. Emotional plasma which can circulate in any system.

A lot of women, feeling that their profiles were too perfect, have had them spoiled in order to give character to their faces. In a world already surreptitiously dominated by women, great beauty could only be a serious handicap.

When water freezes, all the excrement rises to the surface. In the same way, when the dialectic was frozen, we saw all the sacred excrement of the dialectic float to the top. When the future is frozen, or even the present – as it now is – we see all the excrement of the past rising.

The moving plight of the Armenians, who put all their energies into securing recognition of the fact they were massacred in 1915. Their identity is bound up with that massacre, so they have to prove it took place. Which may mean going so far as to risk their lives in terrorist acts to force the world to admit that it happened.

Yet there is something rather tiresome about all this. Identity is useless; deep down it is merely a dream, and making claims on the grounds that you are 'such and such' – and, in particular, that you are dead – is absurd. In the Armenian case, it is tragic, since they are not even fighting for the right to life, but for the right to have been massacred. Anyway, how can they avenge the fact that the whole world has blotted the massacre out of its memory for the last seventy years? What response can there be to universal indifference? Terrorism. A surrealistic vengeance which will itself soon be forgotten.

In days gone by, we were afraid of dying in dishonour or a state of sin. Nowadays, we are afraid of dying fools. Now the fact is that there is no Extreme Unction to absolve us of foolishness. We endure it here on earth as subjective eternity.

The most seductive women of all – those anaemic country women in white Mercedes, with their Hermès scarves, now only to be seen occasionally, at the seaside.

For Kepler, the universe was eternal – there was no original Big Bang, indeed no origin at all except by some impenetrable decree (the question why there is something rather than nothing did not occur to the religious mind; it only becomes a question for the nonbeliever). In its stars, planets and ellipses, the universe is fixed and unchanging. In fact, the universe is a ceremony: its unfolding serves as the model for the microscopic unfolding of our lives and thoughts. Such at least was Kepler's view.

Today, we don't believe this. For us, the universe is no longer eternal, it was born with the Big Bang, and is continually expanding (or in potential recession depending on its mass). This is the picture the facts give, and they invalidate Kepler's view. Retrospectively, we can see that Kepler could not possibly have conceived of the world as anything but fixed and eternal, like the religious world in which he lived. This very constraint inevitably meant his perception was distorted.

But what of ours? Our vision is true because it corresponds to the facts, and facts are our religion. But we can no more conceive the world differently from the way we do – i.e. as continually expanding – than Kepler could think of it in any other way than fixed and eternal. Given this equal compulsion, what is there to say that we are not simply conceiving the world with the same degree of veracity and sincerity as Kepler, but not with any more truth?

We like to think that the world is expanding, but when it comes down to it, perhaps it only has been . . . *since the death of Kepler.*

Whether the universe is endlessly expanding or shrinking back down to an original, infinitely dense core depends on its critical mass (and speculation on this has become never-ending, as new particles are constantly being 'invented'). By analogy, whether our own human history is a process of evolution or involution perhaps depends on humanity's critical mass. Has the species reached the escape velocity it needs to overcome the inertia of the mass? Are we set like the galaxies on an unalterable course which propels us further and further apart at a phenomenal speed or is this scattering into infinity destined to come to an end, and are human molecules destined instead to reverse the laws of gravity and draw closer together? Could the human mass, which grows greater every day, control a pulsation of this type?

Not only have the Eastern bloc countries become the sanctuary of civil society, but they have also become the last refuge of the papacy. The Rome papacy is squandering its energies on intercontinental tours and showbiz; Lech Walesa, by contrast, refuses to leave Poland to collect the Nobel Prize. He is the true Pope, the one who does not leave his Vatican and who is adored at home.

His wife goes to collect his Nobel Prize for him and he goes to place it at the feet of the Black Virgin of Częstochowa. This is the act of Walesa I, the Sovereign Trade Union Pontiff, the man of the Gdansk shipyards, whom the West abjectly worships; we find atonement for all our sins, exaltation and absolution of our privileges in this lowly trade unionist, beatified in the shadow of the Grand Inquisitor. Hence also our homage to dissidence. We feel like the first Christians – how comforting! God has sent us his messenger and we have heard him! (unlike the first time, when Christ was sent). God bless dissidence! Our Pope, the post-modern Imposter, has lost all spirituality and hawks the divinity around the tropics at knockdown prices. He makes peace with his assassin. Just think of it! Rome, the millennial monument to hypocrisy, is dead. All the hypocrisy has passed to the East and the spirituality has gone with it. The old theological power, that of the Black Virgin and the Jesuits, regenerated by communism, has rediscovered all its force in Walesa and Solidarity, in dissidence and pro-dissidence. Let us leave the West, as Kant said, to digest its crisis, this hypochondriacal wind passing through its intestines.

1983: the two events of the year – Walesa wins the Nobel Prize, the Pope pardons his assassin. Hypocritical events. Hypocrisy raised to the power of an event.

A woman spent all Christmas Day in a telephone box without ringing anyone. If someone comes to phone, she leaves the box, then resumes her place afterwards. No one calls her either, but from a window in the street, someone watched her all day, no doubt since they had nothing better to do. The Christmas syndrome.

Entire films – *La Femme d'à côté, Finally Sunday* – have become advertising objects. A whole class, that of a culture crossbred with technological or psychological gadgets – a desire-shaped culture as one might speak of a pear-shaped melody – the class of executives promoted to the expression of their own brains because they have been told their brains are like computers, promoted to being in charge of their own desires because they have been told they each have an unconscious structured like a language. It's all this – this advertising sheen of a whole subculture moved to tears by its own conviviality, fired by the thrill of business, enriched like uranium, embellished with the vestiges of self-management and the stereotypes of communication – which is expressed in Fanny Ardant's pretty face and Truffaut's modernist, self-publicizing style.

Anamnesis, exegesis, diegesis, catachresis – a load of meaningless Greek!
The wise man who wishes to know the state of his soul looks at the half-moon of his fingernails.

Life in itself is not to be despaired of; it is only mildly melancholic. Something diffuse in the daylight, something impalpable as language, gives things an air of melancholy which comes from much further back than our unconsciouses or our personal histories.

The tendency of the whole of contemporary culture to become healthy and virtuous again, to recover its intellectual morality, to revive a pedagogic approach to science, history and democracy. The breach opened up by the years 1960–80 is closing; everyone is gearing up for a high-efficiency perspective which is merely an abreactive defence against the imminence of the year 2000. The long period of blackmail by threat of crisis has begun – intellectually too. Back, back to the middle ground, an end to centrifugal passions. What we had dismantled and destroyed in joy, we are rebuilding in sorrow.

Buto: the theatre of revulsion. These twisted bodies, half simiesque, half reptilian. Perpetually at ground level, tensed with a fierce energy, lithe, inhuman and cannibalistic. There is never the naturalistic plasticity of Western bodies; these are bodies that are masked, sinuous, braced. Their eyes are white and they have the tragic obscenity of monkeys, but the pearly whiteness of naked bodies (only the human body is naked, animals never are and they can only, therefore, serve as masks or metaphors for the human body). These larval, twisted, electric, immobile bodies, but, even then, always in a state of mental electrocution, as Artaud would say; these bodies whose limbs seek each other out, their wily forms glistening between pillars of salt. It is the trick of this contorted, shrivelled, monstrous nudity to striate space, to attract it, to make it laugh and tremble much better than the bodies extended in Western dance know how. Silence too is a sort of nudity, a white, pearly form which draws the ear toward it, in the same way as the smooth, pearly, convulsive bodies attract space to them instead of spreading themselves out elegantly in it. This is the whole secret of cruelty: signs which knot together instead of unravelling and which rivet your eyes to the ground. Instead of occupying an abstract space as Western choreography does, the whole of space has to be repatriated into the body, and the cost of this is an insensate, tortured, but never voluptuous nudity, and hence a nudity that is cruel to our sensual imaginations. And then space too must feel revulsion. That is why the bodies have the whiteness of eyes rolling in revulsion. They are like cocoons, wasps' nests, knots of snakes, wild cats with the beauty perhaps of anatomical models – in fact human nudity becomes once more the expression of a foetal, animal world, or becomes like an eternally open, but sightless, eye. Hands are constantly moving up to the face, as though to tear at it; space is never free, the body is an outer shell, death precedes birth, the blood does not circulate, it rains salt, the whiteness is supernatural. Beside all this, Béjart's work looks like a farandole performed by innocent maidens along the town walls – allegories, phantasias and capering. This, by contrast, is a pure hallucination of bodies, a wild frenzy of feline spirits, the mask and forceps, the spectre of birth.

Water, which in itself is silent, is just waiting to make a noise. In itself completely motionless, it is just waiting to move. Perfectly cold and harsh in itself, it nonetheless has the tepidness of salt and the mineral softness of fabric.

Total abhorrence of dominant ideologies. And anti-gulagism is the dominant ideology today. The anti-gulag priests are every bit as bad as the gulag torturers. The sheep have taken over from the beasts of the Apocalypse.

Berlin.

All of a sudden, I'm right there in front of it, without having realized. A long line of graffiti runs right across it, like the graffiti in the New York subway, like the West's mania for stickers. Suddenly, I have no historical imagination to cope with this wall, with this city cut in two like a brain severed by an artificial scalpel. The buildings which border upon it bear the charred traces of a hot history – cold history, for its part, feeds on cold signs, which reduce the imagination to despair (even graffiti are cold signs; the only funny signs are the rabbits hopping about in the barbed-wire friezes of *no-man's land**).

Impossible to feel the old thrill of terror. Everything is meaningless. Here at the summit of history, dismantled by its very violence, all is calm and spectral like a piece of waste ground in November. Any old abandoned inner-city area would offer the same spectacle. What is striking is the museification of history as waste ground. The men who fought the battles remember them like a nightmare or, in other words, like something which is at least the realization of a desire, but now signs are the real battlefield. It is they that are the conductors of lethal energy, they that electrocute. Today, it is circuits which burn – the circuits in the brain, the circuits in the sensory, loving machines that we are. It is no longer buildings which burn or cities which are laid waste; it is the radio relays of our memories you can hear crackling.

I gaze in stupefaction at this wall and cannot summon anything from my memory. I am as helpless to find anything as those who will look at it in two thousand years' time no doubt will be to make any historical sense of it. Mentally closing my eyes, I see Christo's wall, the huge veil of fabric strung across the hills of California ... Where does this passion to unfurl bands and walls come from – here this strip of concrete, elsewhere magnetic tapes or the unravellings scientists dream of – of strings of chromosomes or the spirals of DNA? In their very hearts, their inner convolutions, things are wound around upon themselves: we should not try to sort out the imbroglio. Here the labyrinth of a city, and, at the same time, the Gordian knot of history, have been destroyed at a stroke by a lethal incision. None of this heals over – but the pain itself is forgotten.

---

*In English in original. [Tr.]

It is the same with that film *The Day After*, which is supposed to inspire a salutary terror. Deterrence against deterrence. The bomb deters; the bomb must be deterred. Well, I am unable either to see anything or imagine anything. The immense *trompe-l'oeil* slides of the Natural History Museum in New York affect me much more deeply. You can feel the chill of the Ice Age in them. Here I feel neither the chill nor the charm of the nuclear, nor suspense, nor the final blinding flash.

Is it not the case that all this is unimaginable? Isn't it a fact that in our imaginations, the dropping of the bomb is a total event, after which there can be nothing, whereas in this film it simply ushers in an ecological regression of the human race? But that is something we already know well. It is not all that long since we came out of it. What we dream of is an event which would no longer be on a human scale: what would the earth look like if we weren't here any more? We dream of seeing the world in its inhuman purity (which is not at all a state of nature), in the state of its formal cruelty. In a word, we dream of our disappearance.

The nuclear starblast is of the same order. It must turn the human into pure glaze and put an end to our crazed, sentimental view of the world. It must bring us back to a pure geology of elements and events.

Can this be rendered metaphorically in images? It is not certain that it is possible to evoke it, any more than we can evoke the biomolecular, that other dimension of the nuclear. This does not trouble us, or no longer troubles us, which proves that we are already irradiated. Mentally for us, all this has already happened a thousand times, and the catastrophe is nothing now but a kind of cartoon strip. To project it crudely into a film is merely a diversion from the nuclearization of daily life – or rather: the film itself *is* our catastrophe. It does not represent it, it does not make us dream of it, but says: the catastrophe is already there, it is already with us, *since it is impossible to imagine it.*

The Berlin wall is a physical embodiment of the fact that the Cold War is over. The graffiti covering it merely render it homage by aestheticizing it, in the same way as a slave might weave flowers about the whip that beats him. It is not by chance that Moretti can contemplate making a life-size reproduction of the wall in the area around La Défense with the assistance of the inhabitants of Kreuzberg. The graffiti have decked it out in the colours of dissidence, that voluptuous mental scenario of a Cold War which is no longer what it once was. One day, we shall have to denounce this mystification of dissidence, in which Western intellectuals jerk off against the cerebral wall of shame and refashion for themselves a cheap *aesthetics* of the rights of man, a sentimental aesthetics of the gulag. In its own way, the wall expresses the end of this clear division of good and evil; it has become the nostalgic sign of that end, in the same way that many a monument and event now merely express nostalgia for history, as many an outburst of anger merely expresses nostalgia for anger. If things have changed, then so be it – we aren't going to go on eternally weeping over an anorexic history, over anorexic ruins.

And all crusades are abject.

'The masks will drop down automatically in the event of the cabin being depressurized. If this occurs, put out your cigarettes.'

Must we really prepare to die in a mask, remaining unrecognizable to ourselves even into the next world?

I think there are thousands of dead people still hanging around on flights because they haven't been accepted on the other side on account of their masks. They go on travelling around in the most awful conditions and we brush up against them without knowing it.

I could never travel in an aeroplane with God, nor with anyone who thought he was God (Verdiglione). It is too dangerous. It's not so much that you might crash as that you might never come down again.

The equivalent of the impossibility of getting to sleep is the impossibility of getting out of it again without the horrors of returning to consciousness. Hence the lustral necessity for some ablutionary rite to rid oneself of that cold morning sweat – which is not so much, perhaps, a secretion as a sudden condensation on the surface of one's body – like vapour on a chilled glass – of ambient anxiety, uncertain reality and the first glimmerings of day.

Depressive moods lead, almost invariably, to accidents. But, when they occur, our mood changes again, since the accident shows we can draw the world in our wake, and that we still retain some degree of power even when our spirits are low. A series of accidents creates a positively light-hearted state, out of consideration for this strange power.

San Antonio: two extraordinary events happening at just a few hours' interval in the apparently peaceful life of an ordinary individual . . . would they not be even more extraordinary if there were no connection between them?

When happy events coincide, that is a happy coincidence. But the co-incidence of baneful events is a happy coincidence too. Every coincidence is happy, for it gives the mind a spiritual pleasure. And, no doubt, the very greatest happiness is afforded by the pleasure which coincidences bring. If not, would it really be a pleasure to be happy?

The infinitesimal play of the laws of physics at the bottom of a lake, in the rotting of leaves and in the gossamer forms of frozen ruts . . . Thus the surface of the pool in the forest reflects the pattern of submerged branches. These go on refracting the meagre warmth of the wintry sun even after the pool has iced over, and thus leave a sunken trace of their subaquatic presence. Who could imagine effects so subtle? And under the pressure of the water imprisoned beneath it, because the sound has no way out, the vibration of the ice runs right over to the opposite bank in a long, wailing cry. It rends the air with an almost animal howl. The wounded ice sends out the waves of its suffering. All around the trees have been cut to ribbons by the hurricane. They too seem to be howling: suffering brings the torments of the animal kingdom to the kingdom of plants. But the snow covers them with its silence. All lying in the same direction, they look as if they are floating down a river. The forest has been devastated by a demented whirlwind just before dawn. No one was there to hear the sound of the trees crashing down, in their thousands, on top of one another. A meteoric disaster ... like the slaughter of a herd of animals. It is as if the forest had committed suicide by exposing itself to the wind.

The futility of everything that comes to us from the media is the inescapable consequence of the absolute inability of that particular stage to remain silent. Music, commercial breaks, newsflashes, adverts, news broadcasts, movies, presenters – there is no alternative but to fill the screen; otherwise there would be an irremediable void. We are back in the Byzantine situation, where idolatry calls on a plethora of images to conceal from itself the fact that God no longer exists. That's why the slightest technical hitch, the slightest slip on the part of a presenter becomes so exciting, for it reveals the depth of the emptiness squinting out at us through this little window.

Dead periods have to be left to take their chances. This goes for the present too, which we should not try to disturb in its melancholy deliquescence. Even in politics – indeed especially in politics – relentless therapy is the worst of things.

This is exactly what socialists practise on the social, ecologists on nature and all of us on a host of defunct ideologies: a relentless therapy. Living on because we refuse to see technology give in to death. Anticipating everything, hoarding everything, because we refuse to see events slipping beyond our grasp. We cultivate the coma of yesteryear. We adore artificial transplants. We go crazy over prostheses. Everywhere this relentless clinging to life corresponds to the emaciation of the original figures of life, to the disincarnation of bodies, to the therapeutic reincarnation of a dead world, a bygone age.

A society which allows an abominable event to burgeon from its dungheap and grow on its surface is like a man who lets a fly crawl unheeded across his face or saliva dribble unstemmed from his mouth – either epileptic or dead.

You can spot those people who live inside their own image by the fact that they always expect to be recognized. It is very strange to move among such people. You end up recognizing them even when they are nobodies. And they end up recognizing you even when you are a nobody. This creates an idolatrous familiarity which is the characteristic atmosphere of intellectual circles. You can make yourself an easy reputation in such circles by affecting this air of anticipated recognition and furtive celebrity which raises you for a moment above the common herd. Without this nudge from fame, intellectuals would have no existence of their own. Without this figurative existence they would be reduced to going for each others' throats.

The great, lethal epidemics have disappeared. They have all been replaced by a single one: the proliferation of human beings themselves. Overpopulation constitutes a kind of slow and irresistible epidemic, the opposite of plague and cholera. We can only hope that it will bring itself to an end once it has been sated with the living as the plague did when sated with dead. Will the same regulatory reflex operate against this excess of life as once did against the excess of death? Because the excess of life is even more lethal.

The intense life of clouds is one of the natural treasures of the earth. One of their more stupid characteristics is that they move in the direction of the wind. But you shouldn't rely on them to do that. Sometimes, as here on the coast, the wind battles against them, without managing either to halt their progress or to prevent them from casting their implacable shadows over the sea and the countryside.

They are not so much a surrounding layer of gas as a coating of flesh for the planet and its obscure palmipeds. From them we get storms, rain, shadows and remorse. Seen from an aircraft they have the whiteness of icefloes, they jostle each other like glaciers, they tear each other apart and have merely the destiny of meteors. But what is remarkable, apart from the prodigious electricity running through them, is the prodigious uselessness of these moving masses.

The shores run together, the waters are parallel. The waters run together, the shores are parallel. A single leaf rustles, the others are silent. Who knows how this dream ends?

He was so thin, so translucent, that he had to pass through the same place twice to leave a shadow.

Living out a destiny of convenience the way others sail under a flag of convenience.

Early morning around the *métro aérien*.

These multifarious bodies with their lazy gait. The opposite of the torment of work – the ecstasy of work. Languid bodies, wearied by a bad night, the night of the sleepless and dispossessed, who plunge back into the same dream for reasons of economy. The radiance of these niggardly lives, swirling around, without energy of their own, wherever the wind blows them, near the square. There's never any night, any winter, any sun, any summer – it is the eternal season of work which gives this immortal gleam to the young women with their tulle blouses and bloodshot eyes. They do not see me. They aren't looking at anything. They are going to their work and they are all the more beautiful for that. It would be so nice to tear them away from the blankness of the morning air and plunge them back into their beds, into their dreams, whose tepid forms their movements have retained. They are the erotic working girls of early morning.

During one night of drunken revelry, Soutine tattooed one of his compositions on to the back of one of his friends. This was before he became famous. Twenty years later, his friend, now a tramp, passed a left-bank gallery where Soutine was being exhibited as a major artist. He went in and stripped off. A rich art lover bought him on condition that he walk around half naked at his villa on the Coast. The man grew old and died. Or was he perhaps murdered? Later, a Soutine picture went on exhibition which had a strange grain to it (not at all like canvas) but which was certainly genuine.

No rain   *no rain*   *no rain !*
                              No rain !
No sense   *no sense*   *non sense !*
                              *Non sense !**

*In English in original. [Tr.]

April 1984.

What can you do with such a brilliant spring? What action could counter-balance this streaming of light and vital heat? Nothing is up to the task, not even erotic ecstasy (for eroticism, alas, is not natural and we no longer go in for rutting, the animal irruption of seasonal moods). Make love, go cycling, write? All these things are derisory when set against the explosion of spring. Only one thing could fit the bill: a total sacrifice, death, a yielding up of body and soul. Not the swoons of summer, but the offering of the first fruits, the heroism of a deflowering of life which will never again have its equivalent in the further unfolding of ages and seasons.

But what if the spring were only a mask? What if all this light, this indolence, this unaccustomed heat were merely a mask? Then the only answer would be to go forth masked* towards that masked nature, to cover our faces with animal finery, to respond with chastity and modesty to the sexual ecstasy of nature, to maintain some irony towards this suspect splendour and therefore some auto-nomy in our domain – for in fact we shall never equal the miracle of the light and anticipated heat of summer in these few spring days.

Nothing in man's nature can induce him into that irrational, excessive act of taking power or of making war except the mask, the figure of the mask, in whose shade he can take up the challenge of a world the truth of which we shall never know, and which is therefore fundamentally a thing of artifice. It is the mask which makes sacrifice possible, which allows us to make war, the mask alone which enables us to engage in politics.

*A reference to 'larvatus prodeo'. [Tr.]

One is never simply the child of a father and a mother. I was born in 1929 just after Black Thursday, under the sign of Leo and the Crisis. These mythical powers never leave you. They manifest themselves in a certain mode of thought, a mode which smacks of the desert but is nonetheless vital, analytical and solitary – Solar Criticism. Born at the time of the first great crisis of modernity, I hope to live long enough to witness its catastrophic turn at the end of the century (if there is a logic of birth and death, as I believe). I have a friend born of the flight from Paris in 1939. That exodus had rekindled his father's extinguished passions. He is thus the product of an unexpected copulation with History.

The glorious anticipation of summer by springtime gives you the urge to anticipate everything in thought. But it is the anticipation which is the thought itself. It can thus come to us from natural phenomena, from sun and shade.

Snow is no longer a gift from on high. It falls precisely at those places designated as winter resorts.

This journal and photography are wonderfully matched in being snapshots and combinations of images. The same is true with women and travel. To such a degree in fact that the whole set of these minor activities (for none of them is part of any general project) ends up by taking on an air of singular coherence. But can this last? Can this be a substitute for the suppression of all projects?

We can no longer say things appear unintelligible because science does not know enough about them. It seems that the more we know about things, the more unintelligible they become.

It is like the expanding universe. The more our instruments penetrate it, the further the limits recede. We therefore have to assume that this expansion, this retreat, is directly proportional to the power of our instruments.

Why was it that the universe wasn't running away from Kepler?

Linguistic panic – *Witz*. Uncontrolled ramification of the corpuscles of language.

Cellular panic – cancer. The bestial inclination to disobey whatever order is in place.

Transparency – the simultaneity of all points in time, space and mankind under the sign of the instantaneity of light. Absolute, excessive crowdedness. That of the Soviets was already unbearable, the electrical kind is even more unbearable. No more surfaces (how beautiful surfaces were in the age of depth!), no more distances (how beautiful proximity was in the age of distance!), no more appearances, no more dimensions. We speak of the proxemics of human relations, but we should speak of the proxenetics of information, and indeed of the whole of electronics, for the two are creating an absolute promiscuity of all places and all human beings, of question and answer, of the problem and its solution. The scatology of information; the dream of absolute conductivity can only be both laxative and excremental.

Catholicism was founded on the symbolic obligation placed upon the Pope that he remain at the centre of the world – in the days when there was one. Today he jets off to its four corners, like a professional: apostolate by jet. He can thus afford the luxury of a failed assassination attempt. It adds nothing to the glory of God, but it authenticates him – as media idol, as a figure in the limelight. It authenticates him as a target, and allows him to target the international community as his audience. He really has become the best special effect of the late twentieth century.

'You should see him at sunset, when the last oblique rays are striking Bernini's colonnades, as he emerges from the great door of the basilica, dressed in pale purple, surrounded by Swiss guards, each illuminated by twenty little spotlights hidden behind the statues. This is the way the Polish Pope hopes to carry the Gospel – in pictures – to the pagans of industrial civilization, who have deserted Christianity, but have also been starved of spectacles.'

You are reminded of the theologians' interrogation of Galileo when confronted with his discovery of the astronomical telescope: is a Mass still a Mass when viewed through this looking-glass? It is true that through our telescopic and microscopic devices we are squinting at another world. The theologians were right: a Mass is no longer a Mass when seen through a telescope, just as a particle is no longer a particle when seen through a microscope. But the Vatican couldn't give a damn. Today, it is the scientists who have scruples. As for the Pope, that Master of the Episcopate has now become Master of the Telescopate.

One day, we shall stand up and our backsides will remain attached to our seats.

'Signs don't come about by chance': the idea comes from an advertisement which has appeared on our streets. Does this mean that signs come about through the necessity that they be obeyed? That without them everything would be but a confused and arbitrary game? Is it the real, then, which comes about by chance? Are signs an inevitable consequence or a pure necessity of life in society? This cryptic little phrase thus raises, by way of a slogan, a whole host of questions. But must it really be questioned?

A sign of life: the moistness of the lips. That's what you do for the dying: you moisten their lips so that they don't feel they are already dead. The pleasure of water on the lips is greater than the pleasure of drinking. The lips, as the Koran says, are our fountainhead. Their tactile pleasure, their perpetual motion. The moistness of the lips is in itself a sign of love, their dryness a sign of indifference and death. An unblinking gaze too takes on the fixity of death. But the eyes must not blink too much, or the lips be too moist. These are the fragile signs of our equilibrium of love.

What goes out of fashion passes into everyday life. What disappears from everyday life is revived in fashion.

'Michael Jackson is a solitary mutant, precursor of a mixing of the races which will be perfect because universal, of the new post-racial race, so to speak. The children of today have no hangups about the idea of a mixed-race society: such a society is their world and Michael Jackson prefigures what they think of as an ideal future' (Alain Soral).

It must also be pointed out that Michael Jackson has had his face rebuilt, his hair straightened, his skin lightened – in short, that he has constructed himself in every tiny detail. It is this which makes him a pure, innocent child – the artificial androgyne of the fable, who, better than Christ, can reign over the world and bring reconciliation, because he is better than the child–god: he is a prosthesis–child, an embryo of all the forms of mutation we have imagined to deliver us from race and sex.

Like dreams, statistics are a form of wish fulfilment.

Manicheism is the irreconcilable antagonism between two forces. Morality is merely the opposition of two values. In the order of values, there is always a possibility of reconciliation. The disorder of forces is irreconcilable.

The preference of young women for older men. This stems from their finding in the men's eyes a reflection of their youthfulness, of their actual, tangible grace. They could not find this in the eyes of a young man, for there it would be shared.

For the man, his love for the younger woman is not in any way a form of incest: she represents nostalgia for an earlier life, the dream of a multifaceted object of purity, her sexual charm enhanced by the age difference. The man could not feel this with a woman his own age who would at once seem like his mother.

Today you have to be into biology or necrology. Into archives or protein. Otherwise there's no point either thinking or writing.

Where are the political transvestites? Where are the drag queens, the hermaphrodites of power? The feminoids of decision-making, the transsexuals of management?

The real drag queens, the ones capable of frittering away power in its theatrical extraversion, of parading it to excess, the present-day Heliogabaluses, dramatists of the mockery of power, just as transvestites are the dramatists of the mockery of sex – are the Idi Amins and the Bokassas. They are the true drag queens of arbitrary rule with no concern either for representation or legitimacy – Ubuesque idols, not pious choirboys like most politicians. Perhaps the Pope should be included here since his worldwide success is also that of a great transvestite . . .

The home micro: the first household appliance of modern times which has no apparent function. In this respect, it no doubt marks the real end of the consumer society.

Burgling your way out of yourself, quietly, subtly, slipping away from yourself as light slips away from a room when night falls (though night does not fall; objects secrete it at the end of the day when, in their tiredness, they exile themselves in their silence).

Grey, still day, like a perpetual dawn. The birds themselves were deceived by it. They went on singing all day, even though daybreak never came.

It is Sunday 13 May, 6 p.m. Is this a good or a bad thing?

As evening comes on, a cold silent wind gets up. All we need is a heat storm to put the finishing touch to the unreality of the season. And yet the birds are singing and men are thinking, on this Sunday, in secret. They are warding off the absence of sun and the monotony of Sunday. They are dreaming of the marriage of sun and sand. They are dreaming of fogging up the mirrors and each shining forth in his own madness. They are listening to a piece of baroque music: 'Whence comes, whence comes such a loneliness?'

We are merely epigones. The events, the discoveries, the visions are those from the period between 1910 and 1940. We live on like weary commentators on that frenzied period in which the whole invention of modernity (and the lucid presentiment of its end) occurred in a language which still bore the brilliance of style. The highest level of intensity lies behind us. The lowest level of passion and intellectual illumination lies ahead of us. There is something like a general entropic movement in the century, the initial energy dissipating slowly in the sophisticated ramifications of the structural, pictural, ideological, linguistic and psychoanalytic revolutions – the final configuration, that of 'postmodernity' marking the most degraded, most factitious and most eclectic phase, the shattered fetishism of all the idols and the purer signs that have preceded it.

Even the great burst of light in the years 1960–80, seen with some critical distance, will merely have been an episode in the involutive course of the century, in terms of powerful new ideas. But a portent all the same.

Might a new event produce some surprise? We can say nothing of this, since archives and analysis are twilight tools.

Computer science only indicates the *retrospective* omnipotence of our technologies. In other words, an infinite capacity to process data (but only data – i.e. the *already given*) and in no sense a new vision. With that science, we are entering an era of exhaustivity, which is also an era of exhaustion. Of generalized interactivity abolishing particularized action. Of the interface which abolishes challenge, passion, and rivalry between peoples, ideas and individuals which was always the source of the finest energies.

It is difficult to find a remedy for our own sadness, because we are ourselves implicated in it. It is difficult to find a remedy for other people's sadness because we are prisoners of it.

My sink is blocked. I pour tons of caustic soda crystals down it, liberally dosed with boiling water. A fierce struggle begins in the pipes between the detergent or unblocking agent and the opaque lumps of organic detritus. A furious bubbling and sulphurous ejaculations bear witness to the resistance of the lumps of phlegm, hair, and excrement accumulated with the hygienic violence of the masturbator. And suddenly the whole thing empties, the sulphurous water seems to be sucked down at supernatural speed into the bowels of the earth. Life can go on.

We recently saw parading through our streets a line of young women who, under other skies, might very well have been crowned with garlands of flowers in the Panathenaea. They were angry young starlets, demanding an end to the need to sleep with the producer to gain recognition. 'Talent, not tits and bums!' It is somewhat troubling to see such a problem carried out into the streets. It is well known that the publicity around such things repeatedly turns against the victims and merely compounds the initial violation with a further violation by the media. Here too, it will no doubt be said that these young women in search of theatre parts are already in a state of advanced prostitution. The fact that they come and offer themselves up to the lechery of the public eye, after having been offered up, against their wills, to the lechery of producers, at least bears witness to their candour, if not to their innocence.

The silence of metaphor accompanies the act of cruelty, as for example with the cannibalistic Japanese who moved directly from the metaphor of love to devouring that marvellous Dutch girl. Or the woman who made a present of her eye to the man who said he was so in love with her gaze.
The effacement of metaphor is characteristic of the object and its cruelty. Words are left with only a literal, material tenor. They are no longer signs in a language. This is the silence of pure objectality.

The body becomes heavier and denser every day. Imperceptibly, almost without changing weight or form, it becomes charged with a dead weight which adds itself to the useful mass of living tissue. It is as though elasticity abandoned it to make way for gravitational force. It moves away from dance and towards heaviness. Away from the original movement and towards death.

Thought can no longer keep itself in a critical equilibrium. It has to be spread-eagled between violent nostalgia and violent anticipation.

Of course we should dream of all women. There isn't one of them who wouldn't be offended if a man didn't dream of all of them through her.

Having a child has become a prodigiously artificial thing. It no longer has anything of the passionately accidental event about it; it has become the partheno-genetic fruit of a calculation of biological, dietary and psychosocial data and you wonder to what extent dream, desire or fatality are still involved. But perhaps the race is losing its interest in sexuality, preferring instead a sort of protozoan transplantation. Leaving out of account that what has been conceived by artificial insemination is very likely to continue its life in artificial intelligence and to die of built-in obsolescence. After the mechanical bride, the mechanical widow. Now every human being is the product of a sexual act, a sexual pact or else we should not be the human race. It takes a sexual copulation successfully to produce a human being, just as, among the Hindus, it takes a copulation between the word and silence for a sacrifice to be successfully carried out.

In a sense the child is indeed the continuation of the species. But in another, he or she is a biological vestige of it. The further we go with change, genetic innovations and fashion, the more unreal it becomes, with each new generation, to put our trust in the processes of childbirth and organic growth. The simplicity and slowness of those things are entirely outside the range of our contemporary experience.

How can we claim to exercise judgement if we have lost a sense of punishment? How can we claim to judge anything at all if we no longer accept being judged? And if we are no longer able either to judge or be judged, then we lose all hope of being absolved or condemned in the past or the future. Now, what can no longer be reflected in the past or the future takes place in a single instant with all its consequences. The Last Judgement becomes an immediate reality. We have right here before us the unchecked proliferation in epidemic proportions of all processes, the multiplication of all cancers on an epidemic scale.

No one recognizes their faults or their virtues when these are stated by another, any more than they recognize their own voices on a tape recorder. The world transmits back to us only the asymmetric form of our vices, as a mirror reflects back the asymmetric form of our faces.

There is a pact of pride in a couple's love, a pact of glory, which is at least as fundamental as sexual feelings. These latter peter out silently in the two bodies, but the pact can only be broken by the spoken word.

If you say, I love you, then you have already fallen in love with language, which is already a form of breakup and infidelity.

If it has been possible to suggest that no event could have a final meaning before history had come to an end one way or another, then any way of giving any kind of sense to an event is a way of putting an end to history.

If every day were a holiday, towns would be more mysterious.

The river of irises: instead of a river flowing along bordered by irises, it is the irises which flow between two banks of water.

Against all our historically-minded culture (out of compassion for our present state), the only excitement is to be found in anticipation (out of impertinence towards our future state).

Infinite spaces (Pascal would have nothing to fear today) have become advertising spaces. It is advertising which will fuel all the sidereal infrastructure of communication. No more silent stars or astrological signs. It is advertising which will fuel the no-osphere. The more we colonize virgin space, the more we enter the blackmail space of the fully developed advertising form.

Embryos frozen, unfrozen and then reimplanted in the mother's womb. What becomes of frozen embryos whose parents have died accidentally? Orphans of artificial insemination? Billionaire foetuses? Fortunately there is a committee for embryo-genetic control and a commission for the ethics of human reproduction. But the orphans of the concept? What becomes of a frozen concept whose parents have died accidentally?

It is grass that derives the greatest pleasure from the wind. It harnesses its frivolous, aerial energy, as the waves harness underwater energy. Grass bends infinitely: it is fickle and useless and hence immortal.

Scene from a dream. Always the same one. On a quiet beach, within a few seconds (with the same hurriedness with which the sun disappears), the signs of a fabulous storm. The sea, all at once agitated by a sudden light, snow-capped clouds, an immense wave which remains hanging at a tragic height, before plunging down upon the inhabited world. This time, it dies as it reaches the edge of the sand. But most times, it submerges the town in a total, silent swell.

One day, I shall sing the praises of the magical valley of Vingrau, the magical combe of Tautavel, the limpid waters of the Gorges du Verdouble, the paleolithic hills ranging high above the vines and the Cathar castles, Quéribus, Peyrepertuse, and the memory of the lions and wild oxen which hunted beneath these sun-drenched cliffs five hundred thousand years ago, and were themselves hunted by primitive man – a closed world – closed then upon its carnivorous finitude, now upon its solar quietude.

The dog going round and round in its cage on the luggage carousel at the airport. He goes round once, then twice, standing proud as a little god in the middle of the cases, unaware of the ridiculousness of the situation. Time passes and no one claims him. Cases disappear, but the dog stays there, erect in his cage, full of dignity (and perhaps crazed with anxiety?). Anybody would have died of shame at being abandoned in such a way in front of everyone. He remains as dignified and indifferent as the lions sitting on the high plateaus of an African reserve, their heads raised towards the setting sun, their regal profiles and lofty unconcern in no way affected by their servile condition. The humans come to stare at the lions, but the lions stare only at the sun. The humans wait for their luggage, but the dog is waiting only for his master. He puts you in mind of Leika, the first dog sent into orbit by the Soviets. She too was put into orbit to await the appearance of scientific symptoms. Perhaps the dog is still going around there with all the passengers looking on, if his master has forgotten him. Perhaps it is simply his master who is there, before our eyes, reincarnated as his own dog?

In any case, the 'baggage claim' scene at airports has an eternal value: after that death which a flight always to some small extent represents, everyone comes to pick up what belonged to them in a previous life. It is like the distribution of what each person will have the right to take with him into the hereafter. And by what miracle do you find the same cases, the same bags you had before you left? By what miracle can this dog still belong to his master when they reach their destination? He alone knows, for he alone has never given a thought to death. Any more than the lions or the giraffes in the reserve ever give a thought to the sequestration or the mocking of their state, which is just as absurd as that which occurs on an airline flight. If they had, they would drop down dead on the spot.

After every flight, orphaned luggage continues to go round and round without anyone claiming it. Or the opposite happens, with some people waiting for their cases which will never come. The expressions of those who are beginning to lose hope are unforgettable.

Yet no one steals anyone else's luggage, for each person is intent solely upon connecting up again with his or her own existence. Who would want to be reborn in another's skin, another's case? Who would want to take someone else's dog? A kind of immunity protects those things that have survived the sacred promiscuity of flight and the taboo of death.

Right in the middle of a Stevie Wonder concert, right in the middle of this musical trance, this electronic night with thousands in the stadium, a night worthy of *Metropolis* with the thousands of cerebro-motor slaves gyrating to the rhythm of synthesizers and all the lighter flames serving as a luminous ovation – a new ritual worthy of the catacombs – I feel a total coldness, complete indifference to this faked music, without the slightest melodic phrase, music of a pitiless technicity. Everything is both visceral and coded at the same time. A strictly regulated release, a cold ceremonial, very far in human terms from its own musical savagery, which is merely that of technology. Only the visual impact remains, the spectacle of the crowd and its physical idolatry, particularly as the idol is blind and directs the whole thing with his dead eyes, exiled from the world and its tumult, but absorbing it all like an animal. The same air of sacredness as with Borges. The same translucidity of the blind, who enjoy the benefits of the silence of light and therefore of blackmail by lucidity. But modern idolatry is not easily accepted; the bodies stay clenched. Technicity wins out over frenzy in the new metropolitan nights.

Growing old is not the approach of a biological term. It is the ever lengthening spiral which distances you from the physical and intellectual openness of your youth. Eventually, the spiral becomes so long that all chance of return is lost. The parabola becomes eccentric, and the peak of one's life-curve gets lost in space. Simultaneously the echo of pleasures in time becomes shorter. One ceases to find pleasure in pleasure. Things live on in nostalgia, and their echo becomes that of a previous life. This is the second mirror phase, and the beginning of the third age.*

Foucault's death. Loss of confidence in his own genius. It is fatal to be an

*Le troisième âge: old age, retirement. [Tr.]

absolute reference. The loss of his immune systems, regardless of the sexual aspect, was merely the biological transcription of this other process. The same thing happened to Barthes when he 'allowed himself to die'.

Sartre was still able to die with great pomp. Barthes and Foucault disappeared discreetly, prematurely. The era of the great literary figures and rhetoricians who wore their glory lightly is past. The more subtle thinkers of the media era can no longer do this. Fulfilling the function of an idol – like the wielding of power – becomes harder in a democratic society, where thoughts are without consequence and events without memory. This state of affairs makes it even more urgent that there be a crystallization in the form of voluntary servitude around a figurehead chosen for his abstract and imperious character – this is what happened with Foucault. But fame applied to a pure intellectual condemns him to disappearance. For thought, the internal scandal produced by its simulated apotheosis is unbearable. Nonetheless, Sartre, who had long since analysed all forms of *mauvaise conscience* suffered less from this than Foucault, who paradoxically felt unloved and persecuted. He was certainly persecuted by those thousands of disciples and scruffy little flatterers whom he certainly despised in secret (at least one hopes he did), and who reduced him to a caricature of what he felt he was doing. To forget him was to render him a service; adulation was a disservice.

As it happened, his death coincided with the high point of the anticipatory, blind admiration for a book which had become problematical in the very fact of the suspense it had generated. Deep down, what did he himself expect of this book, after having toyed so long with it as though with his own death? The latter was a fairly elegant response to the excessive, pretentious fame, with which the mentally deficient burden their mentor – and a pretty stinging denial of that intellectual beatification. It is possible to live with prestige, because that comes from your peers and is returned. But there is no defence against the power others impose on you through their servitude. Even systematic disappointment, as practised by Foucault, does not discourage them. In the end, to escape the dogs, you have to know how to run away – or how to treat them as dogs, and not everyone knows how to do that.

The more imperious, despotic and arbitrary Foucault became, the more his authority in the intellectual world increased. This surely tells us something about the impoverished nature of that world. Perhaps it is not very different from the popular world of rock music. Distortion between intellectual mastery and artificial infallibility, a cult that grows as the authority associated with the sovereignty of thought decreases.

The man this compulsive religion takes as its god is already losing his intellectual immunity. He disappears before his own eyes, like a gambler over-whelmed by good fortune, like idols and stars whose very names no longer belong to them. Any society needs these collective sacrifices, which used to be carried out ritually. Must we stigmatize as contemptible these adulators who are merely the officiants at the sacrifice? The whole process is inexorable. Communities come together to elevate one of their number to the rank of a glorious figurehead whom they will then set about systematically destroying by their very devotion. Only, in days gone by, this took place amid festivity; today it takes place amid boredom and regression. It is the work of despotism and voluntary servitude. It is just that it is more of a caricature when it takes place in the intellectual sphere which prides itself on its freedom of thought. You have to have watched a thousand cultivated minds waiting attentively for hours from deep in their seats on the aboulic silence of the ageing Lacan – the recital of silence performed before those who watched him die – to understand that something absurd has occurred to corrupt that admiration that was the finest of our passions.

Foucault: the obsession with an ever more precise genealogy, the ever more scientific elision of an effect in the present by the exhaustion of a preliminary objectivity. It is like a system of thought that has begun to spin on its axis when confronted with an obstacle it will never get over – it will never jump over its shadow, the procedures that engender it, its retrospective sequential logic. This is the way you become an absolute reference, by connecting up with an inflexible heredity of knowledge, with an authority which necessarily seeks to ground itself further and further back in time. An austere line this, which allows itself neither anticipation nor even a breakthrough into the present, which allows itself no mental infringement of the law of its species, which is that you have to be sure of what you are asserting. This is illusory because no thinking can be sure of itself, nor conscious of its own mechanisms. It must take the risk of what it does not say, rather than simply being so careful about what it says. Even if there is a great objective modesty in Foucault's prudence, his tragedy lies in his never having managed to cross this defensive line, of having walled himself up in his own discriminations, always demanding another power. Foucault put all his strategic efforts into constructing that demand, all his energy, which was increasingly uncertain of its own state, and increasingly confused by the exaggeration of his reputation. He died of that infinite regression, disappeared, leaving us no hope, but leaving little for himself either, on the ambiguous fringes of the very Highest Scholarship.

And yet what are the writings of Barthes, Lacan, Foucault (and even Althusser) but a philosophy of disappearance? The obliteration of the human, of ideology. The absent structure, the death of the subject, lack, aphanisis. They have died of these things and their deaths bear the characteristics of this inhuman configuration. They bear the mark of a Great Withdrawal, of a defection, of a calculated failure of will, of a calculated weakening of desire. They all became shrouded in silence towards the end, in their various ways, and words fell away one by one. One can see no rosy future for their philosophies. They are even in danger, to the great despair of their disciples, of having no consequences at all. Because theirs are subtle modes of thought and ones therefore which subtilize their own traces and which have never, when all is said and done, produced constructive effects (at least that's not the best of what they have done). Those thinkers whose minds were rooted in a humanist configuration, whether liberal or libertine (Lévi-Strauss, Lefebvre, Aron – and Sartre too) survive better. Whether or not they are still alive, they have not 'disappeared' in the same way; they have not been infected with the virus; their works perpetuate them and they bear the glory of those works without weakening. A whole generation, by contrast, will have disappeared in a manner wholly coherent with what it described, what it sensed, of the inhuman. It is ironic signs they have left behind, and the whole labour that is left for those whom they have sumptuously disappointed will be to make positive monuments out of those signs, monuments worthy of memory, of a juicy, intellectual memory, with no regard for the elegance and style of their disappearance.

The atoms of time, which used to be organized into complex wholes, have now shrivelled to form dense nuclei, which it is impossible to cross. Their ever increasing pressure is sending us back to the molecular state. Under the pressure of empty time, we are once again turning into beings who are driven only by speed and aware only of hot and cold. Every being is becoming an infinitesimal corpuscle, but one animated by ever greater speed. Only acceleration gives us a sense of life; any deceleration is lethal.

Let us turn our gaze towards the Southern lands, where only the melancholy light of origins shines.

When you fly over twenty thousand kilometres or so of the earth, you see that it is made up, from Arctic to Antarctic, of a harmonious set of deserts — including the oceans — punctuated by a few strange conurbations and some zones of furious vegetation. Distance is swept away by the sleepless night of the time zones, or by its mapping out as a geometric function, in terms of the multiple coordinates of longitude and latitude, altitude and speed. The bizarre situation of being caught in a storm above the Indian Ocean in a comfortable little pod where the only interesting thing about life is its fragile and involuntary character. There is no sense keeping up any social relations at this altitude. It is enough just to consume your meals while keeping one eye on the ordinariness of these faces with which there is a very small chance death will unite you.

The shadow of the clouds is as fine as a Rorschach blot on the flatness of the desert. The outlines of the dried-up mountain streams seen from a bird's eye view are as clear-edged and jagged; the profiles of the trees submerged by the waters held back by the hydroelectric dam are as exact and dreamy; the racial beauty of the Arctic women and their artificial smiles as they serve you tea in the Southern skies are as light; and the desire never to arrive and to go on revolving indefinitely around the earth is as crazy.

The dream of a matriarchal utopia that is tender and feminine, lethargic and insular – the utopia of Antarctica and the Southern hemisphere. The dream of a drifting continent, where the rules of the game of species and the form of the human and the inhuman would be overturned. Once you have crossed the Equator, the Conscious and the Unconscious should switch over like the poles, all the human constellations should change places like the Pole Star and the Southern Cross. There are traces of this – a whole philosophy of involution and marsupiality. For one thing, the Aboriginals have no sense of paternity (a good sign in a period when paternity, causality and sexuality in general are becoming farcical). The little marsupials are never really born: they climb back into their mothers' pouches and grow up in the open womb. And here even the rivers disappear into the interior of the earth. Even words lose themselves in the interior of language. There is the same foetal tranquillity in the plane, the peaceful sense of being taken in charge by speed, which becomes like a maternal warmth.

The delicious stiffness of jetlag, of the body lost in another temporal hemisphere. A slight science-fiction dizziness, an unshakeable torpor, a weakness in one's limbs – on account of the lack of paradoxical* sleep, the whole of reality is suffused with a paradoxical torpor. For having flown against time, or been quicker than time, the body is struck down by lethargy. For transgressing its space and its territory, it is struck down with amnesia and an absence of dreams. And yet it is a poetic state, a kind of trance, and the effect is like that induced by drugs.

Koala Kangaroo Wombat Lizard Dingo – all lazy, somnolent, maternal or infantile creatures (like furry or mechanical toys). No wild beasts. A foetal, marsupial, herbivorous, idyllic and cuddly state – there is even the shadowy, and lethal, figure of the serpent and a few Aboriginal survivors from the original sin. WOOLLOOMOOLLOO!

Bereft of wild animals and history, but not of myths and wind, the whole bathes in a prenatal lethargy, a sweetness and melancholy which are also present in social life.

Is this our original condition? And supposing it is, what caused things to slough off their lazy, maternal skins, to emerge into the real? You get the impression that a lot of things here have not yet received their septentrional baptism of reality.

---

*More commonly called REM (rapid eye movement) sleep. [Tr.]

*Dreamtime?** The austral Unconscious? Omnipotence of thought over the vast reaches of the desert: the Aboriginal is the only man capable of communicating over such fabulous distances. May there be a connection between this cosmic fable, between this oneiric past whose primitiveness is that of another world and a hypermodern, hyperreal future, between the telepathic ecosystem of the Aboriginals and our White telecommunications system, which also has, in its way, the omnipotence of thought as its objective?

By its remoteness, insularity and ancestrality, Australia is already a kind of spaceship, a kind of continent adrift on another geographic and temporal orbit.

The absolute contrast between the diurnal brilliance of light on the Gold Coast and the Great Barrier Reef, the wintry and subtropical glare of an atmosphere purified by the nearby desert, and the 'faint', the crepuscular glimmering of the aboriginal undergrowth, of the nocturnal mammals, the animals which hunt by night, of the intellectuals cowering in their nocturnal consciousness and the obscurity of their research. Against exposure to the outside world: the pink night of the kangaroo's pouch or of the underwater coral. Everything learns to go underground or underwater, be it into the Unconscious or into the shadowy reaches of books or the dark recesses of the earth; everything moves with a nocturnal slowness and agility, in an effort to survive.

The coexistence – both geographical and mental – of insularity and a fabulous space, of an involutive and an extensive utopia. A nostalgic indecision which affects minds too, caught as they are between a sort of foetal tranquillity and proud modernity. Different from the USA, where this insular form of original reverie is unknown.

*In English in original. [Tr.]

The airiest forest is a forest of eucalyptus trees, which do not give much shade, since the leaves lie side-on to the sun. The eucalyptus sheds its skin as though it were slipping out of a dress and, beneath, it is soft to the touch, like skin. It is a tree that is feminine in its pallor and has great natural elegance. Its leaves make the sky seem deep and light, and there is nothing more beautiful than their outlines against the light.

The more the Aboriginals are exterminated, the more nostalgia for them will grow within Western consciousness, which was already stupefied by them once when they first made their appearance in the seventeeth and eighteenth centuries (the most astonishing moment in our history: just when the West was inventing universal reason for itself, it discovered in the Antipodes a humanity refractory both to history and to progress, pre-adamic and fabulous, which it could only destroy by annexing it to that universal reason – and that left history booby-trapped by murder). It is as if an evil genius had reserved this stinging contradiction made up of primitivism and negritude for civilized arrogance (perhaps it was even, as was said of the neolithic painters, a diabolical invention by eighteenth-century libertines?). However this may be, philosophical and moral consciousness, which was already stupefied by their appearance, will remain paralysed by their extermination. And it will be increasingly paralysed, to the point where it grants them an ill-fated right of veto over its own values.

It is the same with science. For what do we find at the end, what do we bring to light by hunting it down whether it be in the Southern seas or in the field of biology? Always a black object, maleficent little tribes, who would have done better to remain secret, for the greater good of the Enlightenment. It is always the worst that is dug up, and it always ends up taking its revenge.

Lord X, navigator and missionary, setting sail for Australia at the end of the eighteenth century with two thousand volumes, together with hundreds of sacks of wheat which he hopes the natives will sow on the land – they who have never even thought of scraping at the soil to get anything whatever from it, who have preferred to burn it and roam around it for centuries, to the point where they have reduced it to desert.

Of all inhabited lands, Australia and the Pacific Islands are closest to the eighteenth century, because they still bear the marks of their discovery. The Aboriginals are, even today, less near to their origins than to the moment when they were seen and resuscitated by our gaze. They are therefore, with their costumes, their mysterious drawings and their cannibal faces, the bearers of a poetry of the Enlightenment and of all that prerevolutionary period, a role they fulfil better than our châteaux or paintings or the Encyclopaedia (which, indeed, bathes in the glory of their very recent discovery). Deep down, the most original thing the eighteenth century invented wasn't the Enlightenment but the Southern hemisphere, the soft, lunar, maternal hemisphere.

The conjunction of the 'straightest', most austere product of the Northern hemisphere – the presbyterian, the Anglo-Saxon, the quintessential hyperborean, in his pride and his theology – and the most primitive, regressive, impotent and also the most unselfconscious element that the Antipodes concealed under the sun: the Aboriginals. The clash resulted in the quasi-total extermination of the Antipodean, but the Southern hemisphere has not perhaps pronounced its last word yet.

The Aboriginals were certainly had. They were led to claim for themselves stretches of land which in the days when they had been left alone they had roamed through as nomads with never a thought of ownership. Their claim was directed towards an object they had never possessed and which they would have thought it contemptible and sacrilegious to possess. Typical Western cunning. In return they have palmed off an even deadlier virus on to us – the virus of origins.

Ayer's Rock, that gleaming monolith in the middle of the desert, has been given back to the Aboriginals. But with so many tribes – which one was it to be given to? To prove their rightful claim, the Umburu tribe set about dancing, i.e. jumping up and down for an hour, an aesthetically impoverished and unattractive exercise, but it provided the required proof: it was they who were the sacred inheritors of ULURU. And everyone yielded to their claim. Perhaps some day the Aboriginals will give the Sydney Opera House back to the Whites, provided, of course, that they (the Whites) are able to perform the 'right dance'!

These old Australians or Californians who spend all their days staring at the ocean without leaving their limousines, which they have turned into their panoramic childhood sites and their coffins, and who dream there, while awaiting the last wave, the one that will come from the depths of the ocean to engulf them.

In the grey, heavy Bangkok dawn, a dream of the Antarctic, of gleaming white snow, or of that island surrounded by coral, crystalline thought, transparent brain, a lethargic path through the dark vegetation, the beginning of the world, the epitome of life in a single stretch of land jutting out of the sea, in the palm of your hand, in a perfect oval, in the vividness of its detail, in the perfection of its insularity . . . Heron Island.

Asia so degraded, so corrupted by the colonial era and by its own crowdedness that it can only choose between depravity and the puritan orgy of communism.

The women of Thailand are so beautiful that they have become the hostesses
of the Western world, sought after and desired everywhere for their grace, which
is that of a submissive and affectionate femininity of nubile slaves – now dressed
by Dior – an astounding sexual come-on in a gaze which looks you straight in the
eye and a potential acquiescence to your every whim. In short, the fulfilment of
Western man's dreams. Thai women seem spontaneously to embody the sexuality
of the Arabian Nights, like the Nubian slaves in ancient Rome. Thai men, on the
other hand, seem sad and forlorn; their physiques are not in tune with world chic,
while their women's are privileged to be the currently fashionable form of ethnic
beauty. What is left for these men but to assist in the universal promotion of their
women for high-class prostitution?

Having gone as far as you can does in a way put an end to the journey. The
only further stage is never to go back again – to discover the 'distance of liberation'. The further you travel the more clearly you realize that the journey (destiny)
is all that matters. It has to describe an arc across the earth, espouse the curvature
of the earth and attain sufficient velocity to be tempted to escape from it. Thought
too must espouse the curvature of things, their inflexion, their reversibility and be
tempted at any moment to escape to starry heights, for to discover at a particular
moment the curvature of life is no less moving than to sense, at great altitude, the
curvature of the earth.

You have to travel, keep on the move. You have to cross oceans, cities, continents, latitudes. Not to acquire a more informed vision of the world – there is no universality any more, no possible synthesis of experience, nor even, strictly speaking, is there any pleasure of an 'aesthetic' or 'picturesque' variety to be had from travel – but in order to get as near as possible to the worldwide sphere of exchange, to enjoy ubiquity, cosmopolitan extraversion, to escape the illusion of intimacy. Travel as a line of flight, the orbital voyaging of the age of Aquarius.

Philosophy has never been anything but a disavowal of the reality principle. Up until now, it has been the business of philosophers. Today this unreality has entered into things. This then is the end of philosophy and the beginning of something else in which reality merges with its ironic refraction.

Television knows no night. It is perpetual day. TV embodies our fear of the dark, of night, of the other side of things. It is the incessant light, the incessant lighting, which puts an end to the alternating round of day and night (hence the absurdity of a TV service like the French which closes down at 11 p.m.).

There is something of both childishness and sorcery in a woman making up. The event keeps the world in suspense by the simple interaction between a mirror and a face. It is the reconciliation of technique and guile. It has no equivalent in the universe of thought except perhaps when suffering is dressed up in ascetic garb. It is, moreover, each day (and several times a day) the sacrificial moment of a woman's life.

You can only go into mourning by transfiguration or disfiguration. There is no rational form of the absorption of death.

One regresses so far on a flight that it must be easy to die. The infantility carries you straight off to paradise.

The range of compromises
the inanity of discourse
the abomination of the concept
unidentified sexual objects
the stasis of baldness

Just as an excess of pain causes you to fall into a faint or unconsciousness, and just as extreme danger plunges us into a state of physical and mental indifference which corresponds to the brutal indifference of the world towards ourselves, isn't this disintensification of affects (or of 'movements of the spirit') in an artificially animated world a ruse of the species while awaiting a better world?

'Every ecstasy in the end prefers the path of renunciation to sinning against its own concept by realizing itself' (Adorno). Isn't the same true of the social too – a general all-out collusion to prevent the realization of the social for fear of damaging the concept and forever destroying the hopes that surround it?

The pharaonic era of the country-house technocrats. The dream of an electronic control of things runs up against the traditional stupidity of the masses. Collective demand has never been so elicited, forced or violated as it has in the field of computing.

The clash between a philosophical and metaphysical exigency and a present which is no longer in the least philosophical and metaphysical.

The clash between a system of representation and a system of simulation.

The clash between a thinking of difference and a thinking of indifference.

What is the power of indifference? What would an analytics of indifference be like?

Torn between a radical indifference and a radical seduction.

Postmodernity is the simultaneity of the destruction of earlier values and their reconstruction. It is renovation within ruination. In terms of periods, it is the end of final evaluations and the movement of transcendence, which are replaced by 'teleonomic' evaluation, in terms of retroaction. Everything is always retroactive, including – and, indeed, particularly including – information. The rest is left to the acceleration of values by technology (sex, body, freedom, knowledge).

Waiting is an anticipated expiation. Every pleasure is surrounded by a waiting area which expresses the fact that millions of people desire the same thing at the same time. Waiting is the neutralization of the respective desires which bear upon the same object. Even perhaps upon suffering and death. If death were a public service, there would be waiting lists. Impatience finds its justification as a refusal of this void, this abeyance of time which has no justification in any other world and which is produced by the overcrowding, the overpopulation of all desires.

Certain women dream only of winning a man. Others, though they are rarer, dream only of losing men. They have expiated their femininity in advance and the pleasure it can give them. If they have some sensual disposition, this disappears to be replaced by a more subtle game-plan. Just as thought reserves itself a sort of mental domination, with no concern to change the world, but the sole aim of abolishing it, certain women devote themselves to a sort of mental prostitution in which men, weary of tame pleasures, may play at their own ruin.

The Pentagon accuses Texas Instruments of providing it with unreliable electronic equipment. T.I. retorts that testing already eats up one-third of the budget and that it is impossible to test such equipment without sacrificing years to do it, at the end of which the equipment would be outdated (however, it is built to fulfil essential tasks: military defence, nuclear ballistics, scientific calculations). This is wonderful. High technology here connects up once again with the social system, which also can no longer insure against the random consequences of its own functioning. It too puts individuals, laws and products into circulation without having tested, analysed and identified them properly (on-the-job training is a failure). Or else you are tested so minutely that you are, in the end, no use at all, like Michelin tyres after endurance trials. Citizens are polled so often that they now have no opinions left. Like the Dogons who were subjected to so much research by ethnologists that they were forced to invent dreams and rites to keep them happy. Everywhere, the (medical, scientific, military or social) machine goes beyond the possibilities of its object; it is therefore forced to turn back against itself, to lose itself in endless adjustments, indefinite corrections. The countdown gets lost in the ignition checks. The launch of the rocket is postponed indefinitely (in the meantime the cosmonauts have aged, if they have not indeed died of radiation poisoning from the checks). The only advantage: war itself is indefinitely postponed: it has to be tested first in all its possible consequences.

The population, who are, ultimately, indifferent to public affairs and even to their own interests, negotiate this indifference with an equally spectral partner and one that is similarly indifferent to its own will: the government [*le pouvoir*]. This game between zombies may stabilize in the long term. The Year 2000 will not take place in that an era of indifference to time itself – and therefore to the symbolic term of the millennium – will be ushered in by negotiation.

Nowadays, you have to go straight from money to money, telegraphically so to speak, by direct transfer (that is the viral side of the matter). A viral revolution, then, more akin to the Glass Bead Game than to the steam engine, and admirably personified in Bernard Tapie's playboy face. For the look of money is reflected in faces. Gone are the hideous old capitalists, the old-style industrial barons wearing the masks of the suffering they have inflicted. Now there are only dashing play-boys, sporty and sexual, true knights of industry, wearing the mask of the happiness they spread all around themselves.

The world put on a show of despair after 1968. It's been putting on a big show of hope since 1980. No more tears, alright? Reaganite optimism, the pumping up of the dollar. Fabius's glossy new look. Patriotic conviviality. Reluctance prohibited. The old pessimism was produced by the idea that things were getting worse and worse. The new pessimism is produced by the fact that everything is getting better and better. Supercooled euphoria. Controlled anaesthesia.

I should like to see the equivalent of Bernard Tapie in the world of business emerge in the world of concepts. Buying up failing concepts, swallowing them up, dusting them off (firing all the deadbeats who are in the way), putting them back into circulation with a dynamic virginity, sending them shooting up on the Stock Exchange and then abandoning them afterwards like dogs. Some people do this very well.

It is perhaps better to save tired concepts by maintaining them in a super-cooled state like unemployed labour, or locking them away in interactive data-banks kept alive on a respirator.

Everywhere power has to be seen in order to give the impression that it sees. But this is not the case. It doesn't see anything. It is like a woman walled up in a 'peepshow'. It is separated from society by a two-way mirror. And it turns slowly, undresses slowly, adopting the lewdest poses, little suspecting that the other is watching and masturbating in secret.

The metro. A man gets on – by his glances, gestures and movements, he carves out a space for himself and protects it. From that space, he sets his actions to those of the neighbouring, approximate molecules. He becomes the centre of a physical pressure, sniffs out hostile vibrations and emanations, or friendly ones, on the verge of panic. He joins up with others out of fear. He innervates his whole body with a calculated indifference, wraps himself in a superficial reverie, created only to keep others at a distance. He deciphers nothing, protects himself from the crossfire of everyone's gazes and sets his own as a backhand down the line, staring at a particular face at the back of the carriage until the very lightness of his stare stirs the other in his sleep. When the train accelerates or brakes, all the bodies are thrown in the same direction, like the shoals of fish which change direction simultaneously. The marvellous underwater lethargy of the metro, the self-defence of the capillary systems, the cruel play of vague thoughts – all while waiting for the stop at Faidherbe–Chaligny.

The crucial thing is not to have sweeping views of the future, but to know where to plant your primal scene. The danger for us is that we'll keep running up against the wall of the Revolution. For this is the source of our misery: our phobias, our prohibitions, our phantasies, our utopias are imbedded in the nineteenth century, where their foundations were laid down. We have to put an end to this historical coagulation. Beyond it, all is permitted. It will perhaps be the adventure of the end of the century to dissolve the wall of the Revolution and to plunge on beyond it, towards the marvels of form and spirit.

Our leader hasn't got the right kind of smile. It is bringing us a rainy autumn. See how Reagan's smile brings down all the Lord's blessings upon America. There's a good leader for you – one they would have appreciated in a primitive society. Mitterrand's strained smile brings us nothing but water. Even on the night of 10 May there was a fantastic storm. We are still awaiting the Indian summer of socialism.

Neither optimism nor pessimism: they are moral qualities which have nothing to do with the immorality of theory.

For whole generations, a certain pessimism is associated with the historical failure of revolutions. That pessimism is a thing of pathos. The other less sentimental, fiercer type comes from recognizing how ideal things are, the perfection and exactitude of our freedom and the absolute availability of the simplest solutions. For example, the resolution of the famine problem in Ireland by killing off the young children. You could not do better; there is no more elegant solution. It is a stroke of wit. The stroke of wit also despairs of language, but from that despair it always derives a brilliant solution, drawing a line between two diametrically opposed poles. A diabolical simplification; everything is in the ellipsis. There is no crueller trick you can play on reality than to idealize it just as it is. It never recovers from that (whereas it can easily cope with being denounced). Deify power right where it is and it can't believe its eyes. Take the people who marched through Red Square with placards reading 'We are happy in the Soviet Union! The Soviet Union is the land of happiness.'

If you set five men pulling on a rope, you multiply the strength of each individual by five. With death, it's the other way round. If you kill a thousand men, the death of each is a thousand times less important than if he had died alone (Gombrowicz). A specious logic, since it is a matter of quantity in the one case and of quality in the other (the one is multiplied, the other divided, so deep down there is no paradox). But it is a superb proposition all the same!

Certain regimes reserve for themselves a monopoly on physical violence. As for the socialists, they reserve a monopoly on moral comedy. That is why it is quite difficult to make fun of them. But this is not something they should be proud of, because when something no longer makes you laugh, it probably means what is ridiculous about it is already deeply buried away, immune from further harm, irreparable. It is against all the rules for power to appropriate a function – ridicule – which commonly belongs to the sphere of manners and which is normally the province of the public mind.

The United States has a fantastic capacity for absorbing violence. Italy has an equal capacity for absorbing derision. It is a quality inherited from its history. The Mafia: a blood-stained mockery of official power, the ritual staging of its liquidation: popular opera. Will the authorities which have been derided in this way collapse? Not at all. They continue to swing from right to left, on the end of their thread, as if on a piece of old elastic. They survive by the pity they inspire. No one (except the Red Brigades) wants to put them to death. What marvellous wisdom! For the truth of our societies is that they can no longer cut away evil: they have to absorb it. Madness can no longer be locked away; it has to be assimilated. It is enzymes, not counterirritants that must be put to work. Dissolve, dissolve, dissuade. In Italy authority dissolves of itself in scandals, debauchery and historical compromises, but it does so with a certain urbanity, offering the spectacle of its fall and its periodic resurgence. There are very few societies so advanced.

Our societies are changing. It is no longer an atmosphere of repression that weighs upon us, that haunts our streets and our minds. It is the glossy, efficiency-minded atmosphere which is knocking the wind out of us. Literally, euphoria, dumping and acceleration are absorbing all the oxygen from the atmosphere and leaving us like washed-up fish. It is no longer light we are short of, nor cash, but air. The oppression weighs not upon our persons, but upon our chests. Is it the approach of the end of the century which is producing this effect of pumping off, sucking out our air? Are we not just rushing around merely to escape that? In fact we are beginning to mime what we believe the twenty-first century should be, in order to save ourselves the trouble of a lethal transition. We get high on futurology to divert attention from our lack of perspective. We are accelerating in a desire to get past the millennium in fine shape, in an impeccable 'dissolve', unconcerned by that magic date. There are no fatidical numbers or stars any more. The coming years have already been sacrificed. They no longer count. They have already fallen into the umbra of the space ship that is the next century, been obliterated in the penumbra of speed. We shall have trouble hearing the grass grow, the wind whistle and fate being accomplished. For everything is already going under in the wake of this sort of olympian performance humanity is collectively imposing upon itself.

O C T O B E R   1 9 8 4

For difference is beautiful,
but indifference is sublime

The insane hope of being proved wrong: if reality exists it cannot but rise to this challenge, even to the point of systematically destroying its images, as the iconoclasts did with the images of God. Unfortunately, they were defeated, God never rose to their challenge. He's no fool, the Deity: He sided with the iconolaters, with those who did not believe in Him and revered only His likeness. After all the strivings of the iconoclasts, we shall doubtless have to give in to that way of thinking ourselves, and give up questioning a reality which has preferred to disappear, as God did long ago, behind the perfect alibi of images.

There is somewhere a worm teamed up with a symbiotic alga which helps it with its digestive process. This all works very well except when the worm digests the alga and dies because without the alga it cannot digest its food.

The finest witticisms are found in nature.

According to Zinoviev, the consequence of the Third World War will be universal communism as the mode of organizing further life on the planet. From this point of view, the Communist countries appear as Third World War mutants, models from beyond the catastrophe, marked with the ghostly character of extermination. Which is true politically: these states have performed the annihilation of their own societies, destroyed their peoples and reorganized them on this 'transpolitical' basis. We are not far from having done the same ourselves, though by a quite different route. Which means, in consequence, that *the Third World War has already happened,* that it is no use either hoping for it or fearing it, since it is going on here and now around us. This is why Zinoviev's idea of communism is well in advance of all the politico-'imperialist' analyses produced in the West. His communism has nothing of the ideological and the historical about it: it is already a post-nuclear-fusion supercooling; it rules not over life, but over survival. It is of the order of – and has the power of – objectality (as, ironically, does Zinoviev's thought).

Entirely in agreement with Salieri when he rails against God for having given humanity the gift of Mozart's divine music, for the sole purpose of making us look ridiculous and plunging us into despair. Salieri sets himself up as Man's champion against divine injustice. It is the same problem as that of the Grand Inquisitor in the Brothers Karamazov. When Christ returns to earth he says to him: 'We manage humanity for its greatest happiness. It has paid for this with its mediocrity. Don't come disturbing this fragile balance with insane promises.' And he condemns Christ to death once again.

Salieri is not mean-spirited: it took pride, not to become jealous of Mozart, but to challenge God and ask: 'Tell it to me plainly, why am I not Mozart?' For God mocked us by throwing Mozart among us in the guise of a vulgar being, who did not even bear the exceptional marks of grace. God is toying with us, and that is unbearable. Mozart must be destroyed. All that challenges God is noble in spirit and superior to gaping, unconditional admiration of His works.

We will not have the same problem with Changeux's Neuronal Man, emerging on the horizon like Nietzsche's Last Man, with his cortical and synaptic flatness. Farewell Mozart, farewell Salieri, no more grace, but no more challenges either, such is the solution offered by modern science to the insoluble despair of the difference between men.

Signs, signs? Is that all you have to say? People act and people dream, they speak or they don't – none of that is unreal. Shut up and watch. See the philosophical beauty of these closing years of the century, the stars in the sky falling lower as the fateful date approaches, and the interactive horizon of couples in love – all this is beyond doubt, and it moves me to tears . . . The age, the coming age is like a metropolis deserted by its population, cut off from its sources of energy. Are you going to say that, are you going to go on with these twilight rantings? Every century throws the reality principle into question as it closes, but it's over today, finished, done. Everybody works these days.

Narrative and moral passions, the philosophical animal spirits, are literally blocking the electronic animal spirits, a thousand times more lively and insignificant. Videos and advertisements, credits, news reports and sports flashes, *Dallas*, that's television, all that transfers easily, with the minimum of energy, on ephemeral film. But pure television, like pure painting or pure speed, is hard to bear.

The most beautiful woman would be the one I would trace a fractal object for on the misted-up surface of the car window. I would see a fractal love light up in her eyes, a fractal kiss form on her lips and we would leave for those empty Alps, those fractal lunar landscapes which smack so much of mathematics.

Rio.

Not only are the Blacks and the Indians slaves to the technology of the Whites, but they also have to be slaves of their nostalgia for origins. They have to fill the role of ancestor to the human race and bear witness to its mysterious and ritualistic origins. A division of labour: some exploit them physically, while others exploit them culturally, feeding on their music, their dance and their description within anthropology. There is no contradiction in this. Indeed it is quite the reverse: the slaves collude in all this themselves. In hunting, the whole animal is put to use: meat, horns, hair, blood and fur – even the entrails will serve to read the future and the mask will serve as emblem of the deity.

There are of course happier things you can say about Brazil. In particular, that a part of the happiness and the sensuality, the vital languor and the maternal seduction of everything here – in spite of the objective misery – derives precisely from that coupling of master and slave, which extends as far as the abduction of women and vital energy and as far as the absorption by all of the ritual signs of servitude. This is the revenge of the cultural order on the political, something which no longer occurs within Western societies, perhaps for want of sufficiently subtle slaves. Here time maintains a unity, is a time that lends itself to living, in its monotonous, languorous unfolding, the bodies all mingling together, both the master's and the slave's, even though the master tortures the slave and the slave devours the master. But perhaps all this is merely due to the heat.

The heat is like an objective sleep. There is no need for sleep here because it already envelops you like a dream, like a veiled form of the unconscious. Nothing is repressed. Everything is in the insane agitation of molecules. This is the way it is in the Tropics: violence itself is lazy and the subconscious takes on the form of dance. Hence the absurdity of psychoanalysis in these latitudes. It is a parody connected with European privilege, part of the colonial heritage. But in fact, what is the state of the unconscious for us, in Europe itself?

What is fantastic in the baroque churches overloaded with gold and spiral scrolls, with ecstatic figures and stucco flames, is that the artists deliberately confused Heaven and Hell, the flames of ecstasy and the flames of agony. This grotesque confusion is pleasing to our eclectic, or rather libertine, minds, believing as we do neither in Heaven nor Hell, whereas the people of the Baroque age believed very strongly in both and, no doubt more in Hell than Heaven, following a very popular heresy.

A country where shadows do not move round, but merely lengthen and shorten since the sun rises straight up into the equatorial sky.

Amid the luxurious freshness of Ipanema each building has its own secret police.

Brazil plays a sort of giant chlorophyll role for the whole of humanity. It is the planetary accumulator of joy, elation, languor, physical animality and seduction coupled with vital exuberance and political derision. If ever the human race should fall into depression it is there that it would regain its vitality, just as, if it should ever be near to suffocation, it is beside the Amazon that it would get its breath back.

There is no aphrodisiac like innocence.

The speed of things which escape you, suddenly shooting away from you at an incredible rate as if possessed of a force of repulsion, like the bar of soap slipping out of your fingers in the bath.

Nietzsche grappled with the *death* of God, but all we have to deal with is the *disappearance* of politics and history. This disappearance may take on a degree of pathos (as in May '68) but that will no doubt be the last time. May '68 marked the onset of a long eventless process. That is why those who did not live through it can never understand what is happening today in a diluted form, just as those who never lived through the death of God can understand nothing of the convalescence of values.

They are building an opera house at the Bastille. The people will no longer have to storm it, they will go there to feast on regal music. Actually the people will not go, any more than they do now – cultivated people will go, and in so doing will provide a stunning confirmation of the rule that the privileged are always ready to sanctify through art or pleasure the sites where others have fought. The Right is quite wrong to oppose this project: there could not be a finer memorial to commemorate the death of the Revolution.

The night of 'the look' on the avenue de New York. People drift along not seeing each other. It is like a vernissage without paintings. It could be the Exterminating Angel or 'Pure Festival' – pure in the sense of Virilio's 'pure war' – on screen. The only hot spot is the trap-door through which the champagne arrives. Peculiar feverish, power-mad tribe, dissolute yet oversensitive, metaphysics with infrared lighting. Nothing in their gaze, everything in the way they look, nothing in their eyes, everything in the decibel level.

The gentle air of the Piazza Navona in December, with the acetylene lamps and the reflections of the turquoise water on the Bernini horses. A beauty that is purely Roman. In the Campo dei Fiori someone has laid fresh flowers at the foot of the statue of Giordano Bruno, burned for heresy on this very spot four centuries ago. The touching loyalty of the Roman people; where else would you see such a thing? The hot December multitudes spill out into the street: Christmas is almost as mild here as in Brazil. The city is only beautiful when the crowd invades it. So many people on the streets always gives the impression of a silent uprising. Everyone walks along in the luminous muted buzz of voices and the narrow streets. Everything is transformed into a silent opera, a theatrical geometry. Everything sings in this part of the city.

Soirée in Rome. The women are more attractive than the men – they always are. My first impression is that all the men are ugly (they are producers and film directors) and that all the women are beautiful (they are actresses). On a second view: the men are ugly, but they have character; all the women have something erotic about them, but nothing remarkable – a purely macho society, the world of showbiz. The big scene with the male lead is played out in all its grandeur, from one palazzo to the next in the Roman night. The most beautiful actress I know is marrying a rich director, author of 97 screenplays. This is the rule among the showbiz crowd. As usual I feel alienation from all the men there and solidarity with all the women, whom the men pretend to scorn in order to please them, but to whom they are basically indifferent. It must be nice to live in bodies so beautiful, so ingenuous, and allow the men to dominate you with all their ugliness, wealth and pretensions. It must be marvellous to be a woman. Ultimately, it is this which is fascinating: woman is unimaginable. The more beautiful she is, the more unimaginable.

The periwinkle blue eyes of the woman selling jewellery, by the turquoise blue water of the fountain. Tre Scalini icecreams at the end of the day. The bambini with their silver balloons. Mammas with their fulsome familial desire and low necklines. Brothers and sisters embrace beneath the mask of love. Incestuous city, with its domes and obelisks. The very forms of the architecture are incestuous, with their intertwining columns spiralling up towards the orgasm of the sky and the gardens.

A., the victim of her own excessive beauty. Reduced to a state of stupor by the need to let this quite extraordinary beauty shine forth. She seems sad, but is not really so: she simply lets herself be admired, showing no sign of her feelings. Her very laugh says quite clearly: I am nothing, I shall simply be beautiful. In these conditions, can she be an actress? It is true that men love this mixture of hysteria and passivity, of masochistic adornment, when so many other women today use their intelligence as a sadistic adornment. And yet I feel that A. goes too far in her ecstatic submissiveness: she conforms too well to the rule of admiring only herself. How, in these conditions, can she be a psychologist?

Nothing happens with Italian women because everything has been decided in advance, in an incestuous coaxing, an affected vivacity in which sentiment has no part. Games of seduction, courtly manners, libertinism and underlying cruelty. They come to you as though on stage, but they don't know how to weaken. It is they who have driven men into machismo, and who have created all the Mastroiannis of this world. Feminism doesn't play much part in this, even if they claim it does. It is jealousy which excites them, far more than love, the jealousy they arouse, the jealousy they feel continually, with a cultivated excessiveness and obstinacy. They live out their lives as widows, daughters, sisters and mothers, as the whole clan – but never as women. As widows for preference: men they love dead, defunct, suffocating, petrified, stifled by their femininity. By the theatre of their femininity. At five in the morning, all their energies are still being exhausted in trying to give an orgasmic intensity to words.

With women there is neither disappointment nor exception: they are all exceptional, from the moment you ask them merely to be women, that is, to compete with all the others. A lover's misapprehension: the charm of one woman is the jealous absence of all the others – the uniqueness of one woman is the marvellous strangeness of them all.

A society like the Italian, the very disorder of which renders the action of the State useless and ridiculous, is not without its charm and helps us to grasp this political truth: the principal task of the State today is to justify its own existence. To do so, it has to annihilate society's capacity to survive by itself. Surreptitiously undermining all forms of spontaneous regulation, deregulating, desocializing, breaking down the traditional mechanisms of bodies and antibodies, in order to substitute its artificial mechanisms – such is the strategy of a State locked in a subtle struggle with society – exactly like medicine, which lives off the destruction of natural defences and their replacement by artificial ones.

In Rome, Niccolini manages to counter the obsessive fear of terrorism with a cultural revival. To the Romans who no longer dare go out in the evenings he offers festivals, performances, poetry galas. He brings culture down into the street. He combats the terrorist festival with the cultural, advertising festival. He will be criticized for wasteful expenditure, but the only way to fight terrorism is not to create 'solid' institutions, but to put upon the stage a culture that is as sacrificial, eccentric, and ephemeral as the terrorist acts themselves. One festival against the other. If terrorism is a sort of murderous advertising campaign which keeps our imagination on tenterhooks, it can be countered only by a piece of even more effective advertising.

It used to be the Right that was pessimistic while the Left was unfailingly optimistic. Today on the Right it's 'sunrise' neoliberalism and, on the Left, the Tristes Tropiques.

If it is Italian terrorism's ambition to destabilize the state, then it is absurd: the state is already so nonexistent that it would be a joke to try and kill it off any more. Or else it is fuelled by the perverse desire to do *too much* – which might lead to law and order and the state becoming more stable, or at least being perpetually reestablished, fragile as they are. Perhaps that is the terrorists' dream. They long for an immortal enemy. Since if it no longer exists, it is much more difficult to destroy it. Tautologies like these really are the genuine article. But terrorism is tautological. And its ultimate lesson is of the order of the syllogism: if the State really existed, terrorism would make political sense. Since it manifestly does not, that proves the State doesn't exist.

Is it possible to conceive of disenchanted social movements? Yet ones which are still powerful and irrepressible? What would a fundamentally pessimistic political strategy be like, one without illusions, cynical but energetic, one which would transform the fatal state of public affairs into an open challenge, instead of exhausting itself in trying to mask it – unsuccessfully as it happens – though not without making its contribution to turning us into political morons?
We are condemned to a half-hearted, wearisome defeat, simply out of our inability to envisage things without pity, without that sentimental prejudice which

can only produce a sentimental politics. What we need to do, rather, is break out of the psychological poverty which forms part of today's crisis culture, in which everyone conspires in condemning pessimism as immoral. In fact, this immorality is our last chance. But, deep down, why should this situation be resolved?

Perhaps it is better that the political sphere should rot away altogether. We are no longer in a primitive society where the rotting of the body was consciously hastened in order to help it achieve the dignity of death more quickly. We, by contrast, savour the decay, enervation and disgrace of our energies, the fact that they are beyond recall.

The abjection of our political situation is the only true challenge today. Only facing up to this situation in all its desperation can help us get out of it. We should use the energy of catastrophe as we should use tidal or solar energy or that produced by earthquakes. When fossil fuel deposits, stable energies are exhausted, we should turn to the energies of breakdown, to the seismic and the fractal. Perhaps one day, we shall even draw some energy from the night itself? It is the same for mental energies: when the positive energies run out, one must seek an outcome to an event from its taking a diabolic twist, from its maximum disequilibrium, its precipitation. A fatal strategy, but one that is of our time. Isn't energy itself a form of catastrophe?

The automatic carriage-return on the typewriter, electronic central locking of cars: these are the things that count. The rest is just theory and literature.

Space is what prevents everything from being in the same place. Language is what prevents everything from meaning the same thing.

My hand, separated from me, dreams it is holding a breast. Nothing fills a hand better than a breast. Stereotype of a sadistic tenderness.

This journal develops, as its title indicates, over the course of time. However it is haunted by something which preceded it, the secret underlying event.

If the festivities at Christmas and the New Year take the form of an increasingly conventional hullabaloo – since we no longer have the winter solstice as our excuse in the electronic age, nor, in the age of Jesus Christ Superstar, that of the Nativity, nor even that of the snow and ice isolating each person in their own inner space and numbing the blood in the veins – if the end-of-year revels make people so anxious, it is because they are taking the measure of the twelve months that are to come, which they will slowly have to plough through one by one. It is the same with time today as it is with having a child: it is too long in the carrying, too long agrowing. We would like to have the chance to enjoy it right away, to have the fast-forwarded projection of the next century. Think how impatient we are for the year 2000, this whole millennium to get through, while we are already madly curious about the year 2020 and, no doubt, perfectly disenchanted as to what awaits us in '86. The celebrations of the millennium really are going to have to be brilliant to overcome the boredom we feel when we think of the next century.

If only we could at least know that there were merely one or two hundred years to go, that would make things more interesting. There is nothing like a catastrophe to usher in a millennium. They regenerate time in the same way as a cloudburst regenerates low water reserves. Yet it is time, real time, we are going to be short of. If the year 2000 does not happen, it will be because time will simply have disappeared, as winter has in some latitudes.

But this is a dream. I fear that we won't have sufficient reserves to get to this point, and that the year 2000 will disappoint us as the year 1000 did by not bringing with it the end of the world.

One must be simultaneously bursting with life and totally unreal.

Every acceleration produces an equivalent or even greater mass. Every mobilization gives rise to an equal or greater immobility. Every differentiation gives rise to an equal or greater indifference. All speed produces an equal or greater inertia. There is no need to brake. No need for a braking machine. Besides, such a machine has never existed. Only accelerating machines exist. Or ones for decelerating, which amounts to the same thing. But not for slowing down, because no machinery can produce that. Only language, music and the body can do that.

Looking at the material inscription of memory traces from a neuronal perspective, how and where, in which convolutions or in which set of cells and synapses, by what intersection of light and cerebral energy are we to explain the pale afterglow which remains of a dream, this entirely affective mental reverberation of which nothing remains in the memory? How are we to explain that we have in our heads the echo of haunting, precise music, and yet are unable to recall the slightest note or word of it? Or even the timbre of a voice, *but not the voice*? What microwaves carry the traces of a face or of a look which you can *feel* without even closing your eyes, a purely mental image, an image without shape – what reaction or abreaction of molecular biochemistry can account for this purely poetic duplication?

Winter is an emotive event. You want the temperature to fall to −20°C, or −30°C, to freeze the world to the quick and cryogenize it. We no longer dream of the flames of hell; they seem all too naive now. We no longer dream of purification by fire, but of catharsis by (paradoxical) cold. In this age of the tropicalization of manners, we dream of crystalline and deep-frozen forms. As in *Quintet*, that marvellous film made among the remains of the Universal Exposition in Montreal, where the human beings were like stalactites and played chess in the clear frosty light.

Berlin Zoo. The beauty of the animals exiled in the snow, prowling around the artificial rocks as though in the jungle, with a dreamlike slowness, even if this is merely the slowness of resignation. The Australian Aboriginals have this same slowness, this dreamy stillness which they get from the Dreamtime. They are untouched by the frenzy of the human race.

The snow raises the natural darkness of animality to new heights. Whiteness suits wild animals. The morphology of animals is so strange (an elephant, who could have imagined that?) that we have to think that, as Canetti suggested, behind this mask someone is getting fun out of shocking us, is hiding in there in order to hide the truth from us. Such are animals: nearer than we are to the mask or the metamorphosis. More natural and more perfectly disguised. Man has fewer possibilities, either for servitude or for stratagems. He will never have the beauty of a wild beast in the snow, nor the light melancholy of the grey elephant, nor the perspicacity of green ants.

Steigenberger Hof 502. Abflug fünf. Zweimal hoch. Seltsam genug warnt sie mich nach dem Abschluss. Sekt. Wunderweiße Laken. Wundersamer Eindruck: sie bleibt im Hotelbett leigen (wo sie doch in der Stadt wohnt), ich fliege. Da, wo ich schlafen sollte, wird sie schlafen (da wo es war, soll ich werden). Sie wartet doch vielleicht noch. Sie hat dunkle, große Augen, die aber im Dunkeln und in der Liebe blau werden und sich chinesisch verschmälern. Keine Initiale leuchten an ihrem Schenkel – sollte sie mir nicht unterworfen sein? Oder wurde sie nicht erregt? Sie war es, ihre Lippen wurden üppig feucht. Was sie an mir erregt: Befremdung, Simulacrum, Immaterialität. Was mich an ihr erregt: milchige Haut, anschauliche Karnalität. Ich kam mir vor wie Arthur Miller in den Armen Marilyn

Monroes. Süße Tänzerin, süße Performanzerin, süße weiße Hündin. Im Grunde hat sie mich verführt. Als sie im Loft ihr Arm zärtlich von hinten mir um die Schulter legte, wußte ich von vornherein, nach drei Jahren, daß sie da war. Wortlose Vertrautheit. Es lief alles schnell, wie in einem Polaroïd, besser nicht fragen. Ihre Haut war wie zarte Filmhaut, und ich zerriß ihre Wangen wie ein zartes Stundennetz.*

With certain women, we do not love them as we would wish or as they would wish. We prefer to violate them and lose them.

The surprises of thought are like those of love: they wear out. But here too you can carry on for a long time doing your conjugal duty.

Rome, Berlin, Sydney, New York, Rio. My secretarial staff is expanding. My rainbow too. The night which would fall simultaneously on all the cities of the

---

*'Steigenberger Hof 502. Flight departure five. Two floors up. Oddly enough she warns me after settling up. Champagne. Miraculously white sheets. Miraculous impression: she remains lying on the hotel bed (even though she lives in the city), I fly. There, where I was to sleep, she will sleep (there, where Id was, Ego shall be). Perhaps she is waiting there still. She has large, dark eyes, but in the dark and in love they narrow, Chinese-like, and become blue. No initials gleam on her thigh – was she not to submit to me? Or was she not aroused? She was, her lips became sensually moist. In me she is aroused by: strangeness, simulacrum, immateriality. In her I am aroused by: milky skin, demonstrative carnality. I felt like I was Arthur Miller in the arms of Marilyn Monroe. Sweet dancer, sweet performer, sweet white bitch. In truth she seduced me. When she tenderly laid her arm around my shoulder from behind in the loft, I knew straight away, after three years, that she was there. Wordless intimacy. It all happened quickly, like in a polaroid, better not ask. Her skin was like a delicate film, and I tore up her cheeks like a delicate net of hours.' In German in original. [Tr.]

world has not yet occurred. The sun which would illuminate all the cities of the world at once has not yet risen.

Every woman is like a timezone. She is a nocturnal fragment of your journey. She brings you unflaggingly closer to the next night.

Some women have disguised themselves as Congolese dugouts or Aleutian pearls. Why shouldn't they disguise themselves as a timezone, or even as the ecstasy of the journey? Everywhere there is pleasure you will find a woman in disguise, her features lost or metamorphosed into the ecstacy of things. Everywhere there is a woman dying.

The oh so strange story of the two cars concertinaed into each other on the motorway at dead of night. The two drivers were killed outright – they were husband and wife. There is something of the stories of Alphonse Allais (*Un drame bien parisien*) in this odd coincidence: they rush to tear off each other's masks and yet neither turns out to be who the other thinks they are. What is astonishing in this unusual case is the extreme improbability of such a strange accident involving husband and wife and, at the same time, the very high probability of such an encounter (husband and wife are just the people to rush to meet one another). It is like an episode one has already experienced, something totally obvious for the imagination. It's like when zero comes up thirty times in a row at roulette. What we find most compelling in a sequence of such beauty is the sight of the order of the world laid out in all its rigour, and not just in feeble probabilities. Any road accident is the product of a vague series of coincidences, and yet those others are mere accidents. This one is a crime, though not exactly a crime of passion. No one will ever know whether the woman, knowing her husband was having an affair in the nearby town, set out to catch up with him and, by mistake, in her highly emotional state, took the wrong motorway slip road or, again, whether, knowing that he was himself coming home, took the wrong turn with the intention of crashing head-on into his car – but how would she have known that one was his (on the other hand, on that deserted road at two in the morning, and knowing the time of his departure, it was likely that it would be) – or, lastly, whether she deliberately committed suicide, simply choosing any old car that happened to be coming along.

It is forbidden to unplug yourself, and not only in active, interactive social life, but also on your deathbed: it is forbidden to tear out the tubes, even if you want to. And this is not criminal because it is an attempt on your own life – who cares about that? – but because it is an attempt on the life of medicine, and of high technology, which must ensure their own salvation first. The network principle carries with it the absolute moral obligation to remain plugged in.

Terror is as much a part of the concept of truth as runniness is of the concept of jam. We wouldn't like jam if it didn't, by its very nature, ooze. We wouldn't like truth if it wasn't sticky, if, from time to time, it didn't ooze blood.

Verifying to the point of dizziness the useless objectivity of things: science.
Verifying to the point of dizziness the useless subjectivity of desire: sexual liberation.
An object in which there is nothing to see.
A body in which there is nothing to desire.

There is a particular grace in indifference to one's own life and the admission of that indifference is touching, just so long as you are told with tenderness: I am incapable of loving you, rather than being told 'I love you', with all the affectation appropriate to such a statement. There are indeed certain women who can only love in proportion to the degree of boredom they feel with themselves: with them, above all you must not bring them out of their boredom. There is, however, a great difference between real and affected indifference: only the former touches us. But it is very rare, almost as rare as beauty or madness.

There is no sense in refusing honours. That is in fact to do them too much honour. The only strategy is to act so that they never weigh upon you.

Your delicious (and malicious) certainty that you are a beautiful woman only subjugates yourself. How is one to approach her to be subjugated oneself?

It seems difficult to meet the woman of your life when you have several (lives). In fact, as soon as you have a double life . . .

Popular fame is what we should aspire to. Nothing will ever match the distracted gaze of the woman serving in the butcher's who has seen you on television.

With their feet caught in the ice like the pink flamingos, they still thought they were God's gift to mankind.

Humanism pretends to regard the savage and the primitive races as fully fledged beings and even as superior beings (by their authenticity). But the first humanists, the real ones, those we are all descended from, regarded the Kanakas as macaques, grounding the definition of humanism upon rigorous discrimination. It was not a matter of racism, but of discernment. And the macaques returned the compliment, referring to themselves as the only 'men'. The current version, which is moving towards the recreation of a conviviality of the human race on a basis that is both biological and sentimental, is certainly the poorest yet.

We are always distant in some way, in some particular, from our sorrow. Only hysteria can create total sorrow, but even this, once it is articulated, is no longer so bad as it was before. For the same reason, absolute happiness is impossible and those who speak of it must be regarded as hypocrites. In the wretchedness of his New Delhi room, weeping hot tears (no doubt more for the personal offence he had suffered than for the lost object), S. still finds the strength to photograph his telephone.

Since it is the main virtue of the sexual act to raise the body to that exceptional state which is nudity, it is superfluous if that nudity has now become something obvious. That is why love is only beautiful with a shy body, a sex which makes a play of its shyness. That is why it is only really beautiful the first time.

A negative judgement gives you more satisfaction than praise, provided it smacks of jealousy.

They had taken out such a good insurance policy that when their house in the country burnt down, they were able to build another one older than the first.

The unconscious is very serious today – even a little bit sad – because we repress serious things into it: sex, death, libido, desire. But if it were irony and offhandedness which were repressed, what form would the new unconscious take then? It would become ironic; we would have ironic, breezy drives and fantasies, which would surface in our dreams and our slips, in our neuroses and madness. But isn't it already that way, in a sense?

Television will perhaps only have been invented in order, by a delectable detour, to give back its force to the silence of the image.

We certainly have to accept an authority, but one more stupid than ourselves. That is the great law of the political world. This is wonderfully apparent in the USSR (Zinoviev tells of the pharaonic stupidity of the Soviet leaders, equalled only by the pharaonic servitude of the Soviets themselves), but you can see it in France just as clearly. Why prefer Marchais, Le Pen, Chirac and other such hollow figures to more sophisticated people? Why have they not long ago sunk beneath their own idiocy? The fact is that these figures are the surest remedy against the anxiety we all feel at the reign and the primacy of intelligence. They reassure us about our own stupidity, and this is their vital function as it was that of the shaman. And how can you ward off stupidity, if not by a greater stupidity?

I notice that on windows which have been left untouched, which have not, in other words, seen the faintest shadow of a duster for ten years, there is not more than a fraction of a millimetre of dirt and dust. No more, in the end, than the wind and rain scratch from the surface of a rock in the same period. There is a dreamlike slowness to both erosion and sedimentation.

He didn't like his nose: so he gave it to the plastic surgeon for treatment. He didn't like his soul: so he entrusted it to the psychoanalyst for treatment. But the worst was that he didn't like his zodiac sign. He would have so much liked to be Scorpio, Virgo or Cancer. Any sign but his own, since he is always in a negative conjunction with those he loves.

Sign, oh voracious sign, what can I do with my sign?

Fortunately, there is the World Clinic of Zodiacal Face-Lifting, where you can be given a new horoscope and a new hour of birth (though don't ask how it's done). They give you a brand new sign; this is the clinic of destiny.

Sign, oh fatal sign, it is you who change and I am nothing.

But with a brand new destiny you have to be extremely careful. With a new sign, the transplant is delicate. You have to be very careful of your ascendant and not change it too often. Above all, you must never walk about naked beneath your sign.

Sign, oh voracious sign, you are devouring carnivorous society.

They say that stupidity is a crime, but it seems to me that explanation is the real crime. I understand very well when things are explained to me, but deep down, I am at one with those who will never understand. A brute slumbers within me who sneers at such understanding and doesn't give a damn for intelligence. With those who understand, I make a contract of intelligence, but with the others, at the very same instant, I secretly make a pact of stupidity. The intellectual or the person who claims that title (there are no others) is the one who has broken that pact of stupidity, and feels released from it. In so doing, he plumbs the very depths of stupidity.

You can talk of things so much that they end up materializing in your life: simulation, seduction, reversibility, indifference. Gradually, life comes to resemble a montage of all these things, in a floating circulation of women, concepts, dreams and journeys.

In this way, writing ends up preceding life, determining it. And life ends up conforming to a sign which was initially quite cavalier. This is no doubt why so many are afraid to write.

An anomaly in the genetic code of slipper animalcules is announced. A hard blow for the champions of the code. But if the code is no longer universal, isn't this because it is no longer fashionable today to aspire to universality? The idea of genetic code is also going through its agonizing phase of revision, adjusting itself to a new scientific 'look'. The only winner now is the code of fashion, which lays no claim to universality.

A more vertiginous hypothesis: DNA *was* a universal and an invariant, but, once unmasked, so to speak, it has begun to change in order to throw the researchers off its track; it is deuniversalizing itself to muddy the waters. Out of spite or malice, or simply by adaptation, in the way bacteria adapt to antibiotics. We mustn't underestimate this capacity 'objective' processes have for playing hide-and-seek with science. You understand nothing of science, nor of its failures, if you don't take into account this ultimately quite natural evil genius. If all human and animal species change their behaviour under observation, why shouldn't the same thing happen at the level of molecular species?

In its way, science will have achieved the utopian goal of reason, which was to transform the world into a subject. It has become a subject, though not in the way intended: science, by its unyielding pursuit of the world, has awakened in it a malign subjectivity. It has roused it from its slumber just as Egyptology roused the pharaohs from millennia of lethargy. Since then, they have repeatedly wrought their vengeance. It is quite possible that we are unleashing similarly unforeseeable processes (and our new illnesses are the new forms of these) by forcing the object to flee and metamorphose in all directions, adopting previously unknown viral strategies, by having wrenched it away from its strategy of shade and slumber.

Here, more or less, is the present philosophy: a cop beats up an immigrant in a police station – an incidental news item. But this cop had psychological problems – that is a social fact. How can society delegate the exercise of legitimate violence to individuals who are human, all too human, and whose psychology we have recently discovered – cops? This is a real problem (for journalists). The immigrant is beaten up and forgotten – he is not part of the social. The social begins with social psychology and that is always the psychology of the cop.

We see the same conversion in the Greenpeace affair: the fact that French agents went off to blow up and sink a troublesome ship is something to be hushed up. But that there were members of these same secret services willing to betray the operation and give information to the press, that is the real problem, and we shall have to act.

How nice it would be to see the sun in profile.

A ten-metre-high underwater wave breaks over us, and another one comes to meet it. The two waves converge and carry us off. We come out alive though, landing up on a hillside among the undergrowth. This nocturnal wave is familiar to me, in one form or another. It comes back to engulf me at regular intervals, though I hadn't seen it for a while (but since there's no sense of time between dreams, it is always as though I had seen it the night before). No wave, no swell is so fine as that black, liquid oceanic wall coming to enshroud me. Its crest is often luminous and meaning has it none. I don't care what I'm told about its meaning, it's the fact of its occurrence which is marvellous.

Simulating enzymes. They create false biological events. They simulate a virus, a viral attack, thus triggering a reaction from antibodies, though since these have no target, there being no virus to destroy, they turn back against their own source. Let us celebrate this irruption of simulation within biology and wait to see where it will lead.

Have you noticed that flies and wasps die off less and less in winter? It is snowing outside, but the fly still goes to warm itself against the window, out of habit, since it only knows the summer. Even the youngest, born in autumn, still come and place themselves against it. In the same way, they still persist, in modern flats, in circling around for hours on the ceiling, around an imaginary light-fitting. They thus forget to die and this is worrying, for if flies lose the sense of winter, what is going to happen? The absence of cold in winter has already been threatening cypress trees with a disease akin to leukaemia. The black flame of the cypresses was getting lost in the sameness of the seasons. Fortunately, this year, a glacial winter, which followed a scorching summer, saved them from the disease.

The body seems forever a place for subcontracting out psychological problems. My back hurts, I've got toothache, I've got an ulcer, I've got cancer ... what am I subcontracting out in all this? The only justification for the body now is to transcribe changing psychological states. It is merely a pathological indicator light. Only its illnesses have any meaning. It is left to do all the dirty work.

The very term sexuality is a kind of surgical operation (François George). A castration of the body by its operational designation. The very term communication ... etc. A bachelor machine capable of absolute parthogenesis (state of the art).

After an era of lunar mortification, we are entering an era of solar mystification.

Every great thought is of the order of the lapsus. When Benjamin pronounces this terrifying sentence: 'Fascism is made up of two things: fascism properly so-called and anti-fascism', is this not thought sliding, letting itself slide beyond truth, into the fundamental ambiguity of discourse, an ambiguity far greater than any political or ideological explanation, and which alone explains why there has never been any plausible explanation of fascism, whilst anti-fascism is self-explanatory?

Whatever hypothesis you propose about it, fascism poses more problems than anti-fascism. From the very start, it is more interesting than – and itself encompasses – anti-fascism. This is what Benjamin's statement is saying. And it should not be made to say what it is not saying. Though it surely will be.

I no longer even need a window to follow the journey. I can narrate it to myself hour by hour, live it from memory, all of it – canyons, towns, the reflection of the clouds in the rivers. Memory has taken on wings and speed has become an inner quality. A pity.

No doubt it was better that this purely fornicatory and imaginary relationship, with her sexual voracity and her ankle bracelets, which we carried on all over the place – in the Badlands, in the Chelsea Hotel, in motels, in the sand, between the sheets – and which always meant immediate lovemaking in the minutes that followed, never satisfied, but just as sweet, and flexible and blonde, her eyes raised like a slavegirl's and her hand outstretched towards her sex, she free and servile, feminine and muscled, laughing and admiring, animal blood and metallic eyes – it was natural that this relationship should finish with a pathetic fellatio on a motel balcony, in the morning mist and a hypothetical child which no doubt was not mine and which I shall never see. I have even forgotten her name, but I have not forgotten the straw scent of her sex, nor the twenty-dollar bet on salt or snow, nor the sudden menstrual nosebleed I had one morning when I saw her arriving at my place in all her Californian splendour.

*Winchester Story.** The daughter of the famous Winchester, heiress to 15,000 dollars a day, heard a prediction that she would die when her house was completed – just revenge for the thousands of victims which the only too famous carbine had created in the West over a century. Then, like Penelope, she began to build a house without end, interminably adding bedrooms, staircases, annexes. She died in the end, in the 1930s, leaving behind this monstrous 150-bedroom house as a memorial to the holocaust of the nineteenth century.

Before me a scholarly man, of European culture, head of a literary department in one of the great universities of the West. He speaks of it with bitterness, as do almost all his colleagues. Culture is not what it was and he has not the slightest regard for mass culture. He comes from New York and, deep down, he despises California, his colleagues and the decline of standards. He gets 60–80,000 dollars a year and does not have many students or friends. He has lots of ideas, is sincere, proud and awkward. His secret is his python. I see him plunge his gloved hand into its glass case and stroke the reptile's head, which shoots out a voracious tongue and uncoils itself, still famished though it has just devoured a rat. We discuss the diet of snakes. A tortoise slumbers by the fireside in the glow of an

*In English in original. [Tr.]

artificial wood fire. It is Sunday in Santa Monica. Towards four, the sun drives away the mists of the Pacific. But the snake knows neither night nor day; he is immortal and poisonous and, in the words of the poet, he dreams on the hills of the sky. Which is something his master does not do, he whose reptilian brain identifies with the snake's, and who stares long and hard into his face, even though ordinarily he is incapable of looking people straight in the eye. A perverse couple, the somnambulism of the intellectual mingling with the inner night of the reptile.

Melrose Avenue, Santa Monica – Dialogue on a terrace.
SHE: *You are jealous? Are you jealous? You are fucking jealous! . . . Let me say . . . You're twenty and I am forty-two, and I'll give my fucking ass to fucking anybody . . . Do you know that?**

He gets up, crosses Melrose for no reason, comes back, kneels down in front of her (younger, but as theatrical).
HE: *Do you love me? Do you love me?*
SHE: *Yes . . . Yes, I love you . . .*

The Italian kneads his meatballs. An Indian is playing a video game and its shrill soundtrack provides a backing to the conversation. The woman herself speaks in a shrill, hysterical voice. It is pleasant in Los Angeles in November, on the Melrose terrace, around the middle of the night. Everyone is smiling somewhere. No passion. A scene American-style.

The waiter takes the car keys and drags off the woman, who shows off her black-stockinged legs and pretends to be mad.

A black man gets up and, as he passes, says to me: '*Too much love!*'

*Italicized parts of this paragraph in English in original. [Tr.]

Gliding along the road that runs beside the coast in a black Porsche is like penetrating slowly into the inside of your own body.

How can one regret the absence of the other while at the same time feeling a sense of deliverance from their presence? But language itself tells us how: *Regretter la présence de quelqu'un* means both to feel regret that they are there and to be sorry they are not. *Regretter son absence* means to feel regret that he is not there and for the time when he was not there. The melancholy of parting brings on this emotional confusion.

It is true that presence is less delicate in its effects than absence. It is true that it is rare to be able to dream of someone in their presence. To touch them and dream you are touching them. To talk to them and dream you are talking to them. To look at them and dream you are looking at them. Now, the presence of the other has to be like a dream. Otherwise it becomes unbearable. Pure presence is unbearable.

Borges – his blind face like an Aztec woman's, that old shyster of metaphor, across whose open eyes pass flashes of magnesium without affecting him. The blind always seem to be holding their heads out of water. Yet they are gifted in unreality and cunning. I am sure he knows down to ten people how many are there to hear him, simply by listening, by sensing. The lecture is hopeless, but it is a sacrificial ceremony. The listeners are overwhelmed by the intelligence of this man whose cunning ploy is to make it seem as though he were speaking from beyond the grave, as if he were already dead. His muffled, syncopated, barely audible voice condemns the others to silence in the same way as he is condemned to the night. All the metaphors he uses are those of the night, including the thousand and first night, the finest since it is one added to eternity. He is without doubt also in his eighty-four-and-first year – i.e. he has one foot in eternity. There reigns all about him an ironic and cruel affectation. I don't know what animal he resembles. He has a soft spot for the tiger. Put a tiger in your library and take away its sight: that's Borges. In this vegetation of Californian academics' soft encephalons, his silences carve lethal spirals. Since he can no longer see the world, he quotes it. His speech is one long quotation. *'Life itself is a quotation'*,* he says.

The girls, their feet in the cold water, utter cries like a seagull's. Moreover, they are immediately transformed into seagulls, and these in turn into the obscure object of desire, swaying and waddling like the ostrich at the end of Buñuel's film. The summer has arrived.

I was very anxious she might be disappointed and I could never have forgiven her for that. I shall never forgive anyone who passes a condescending or contemptuous judgement on America.

They are at the centre of the world and they don't know it. What they prefer is to be at the centre of books and the earth.

Only sequoias have the heroic, fabulous, antediluvian stature of the first days of the world, being contemporary with the great prehistoric animals. And indeed their scaley bark resembles a carapace. They are the only trees on a par with the geological and mineral scenario of the deserts. After them it is the little species that have triumphed.

*In English in original. [Tr.]

Even in a very large bed she sleeps on the outer edge and her light body leaves no trace. I cannot succeed in taming this fragile, distant body.

I am entitled only to brief embraces with very long gaps between them, and then her legs still remain tightly closed. She does not kiss me, nor does she caress me. And yet there is something tender about her, something animal, rascally.

She often speaks in a very great hurry, as if to finish her sentence before she becomes afraid. She doesn't know how to show she is in love, and indeed she isn't. She likes to be seductive, laughs a lot in company and at those times I no longer exist for her. She plays at emphasizing distances. I don't know how to violate her, and I no longer have the courage to. There is no solution to this situation.

From time to time, I no longer feel she is near. Literally, I turn around with the feeling that she's gone and she has indeed disappeared. It is a little bit like the story of the conjuror who, alerted by applause, turns round and notices that the woman who had been standing nearby has vanished. When I touch her, it is to make sure she exists. Then there will be a glance and then, if I am infinitely patient, a body and perhaps even some pleasure. But, instead of bringing us together, this quite unlikely eventuality immediately creates a gulf between us.

As soon as anyone else is there, she becomes hostile, contradicts me on every topic and wants nothing to do with me. She doesn't want to seem attached to me – which she isn't. She isn't attached to anything, not even to her body, supple and seductive as it is. Physically retractile, she is all the more provocative with it for that. She stammers sometimes, reflecting a timorous show of aggression and a sudden withdrawal into herself.

She is made to be hugged and cuddled, but she doesn't want to be. She wasn't able to bear a child for the man she wanted to give one to, but she did succeed by magic in causing the death of the child he had with another woman. At heart she is a virgin, but a woman's virginity remains an adorable asset.

She does everything with lightness and grace. I love this negative grace, but every sexual exploit is a desperate act with her (they say that of the sexual act in general but I've never believed them).

She does everything grudgingly, defensively. Even the way she speaks. The sentence rushes out to escape you; it is punctuated with a light, high-pitched laugh to put it out of harm's way – the sad, rippling laugh of a nymph, a laugh of artificial and unhappy jollity.

She takes herself for Mary Stuart or Mary Shelley, and no doubt she is. She doubtless dreams of being beheaded in a low-cut red dress. It's that or nothing. Most of the time, it's nothing. She only accepts what can seduce her; she refuses what gives her pleasure. She wants neither to be made love to nor photographed. These are indiscreet acts; what she needs are passion and delicacy, and perhaps something else, which she will never ever say.

The only time I took photos of her, one wonderful day on the beach, quite inexplicably, when it was developed, the entire film came out blank. She didn't want to be photographed and she wasn't. It is an aspect of her sorcery. Her art is the art of disappearance. Or else she exists so little that she doesn't even leave an impression on the film.

Her face is still turned away; she is absent on the pillow as though she were being made to take her pleasure in spite of herself. A feline, contradictory dance to escape one another, particularly at night, a time when body movements end up responding. A foot which moves brings a change in the other's breathing, a negative electricity connects the two bodies even in their sleep. It is similar to what occurs in the Chinese version of shadow-boxing, in which the bodies are scrupulously careful not to touch one another, while at the same time moving as closely as possible to each other, so that they trace out, after all, a space of love, but one which no one dares to cross. Since I have sworn to myself I will not start anything without some sign of affection, some mark of weakness, we are now truly distant from each other, and I no longer touch her. An odd situation: the first one who breaks the silence is lost, the first one who breaks the ice loses face. The situation has something of impossible rape and silent challenge about it. In the absence of any violent scene (you don't travel ten thousand kilometres to spend your time making scenes), we are undoing one by one all the ties that bound us, without breaking a single one. The hardest thing will be to carry this difficult ceremony through to the end and to bring it to a close without a row. For nothing is said (we are both very good at discretion). It is as if none of all this existed. Nothing, absolutely nothing, separates us. Behind this façade of indifference, I am perhaps a monster of tenderness and she a monster of sensuality? Or the other way round. Who knows? This will end perhaps in another world or in a previous life with an orgy or a delicious emotional chaos. But for the moment we are more like Tristan and Isolde. Between us God has placed his sword as a sign of chastity.

Since she left ten hours before, she is already on the other side of the night. I am just about entering the night, but she is already coming out of it, somewhere off Iceland. Thus, at this very moment, we are separated by the geographical space of a night. Many other nights have separated us, which had nothing geographical about them. This last nocturnal separation by timezones is, happily, a poetic one and redeems the others. At least we managed to carry off this night, this last night.

The ghostly movement of the Parisian tribes. Watch the crowd rushing out in the (cold and rainy) spring night towards the urban deserts of La Villette to attend the inaugural cult of the Biennale and then, when that is ended, flowing back in great waves towards the inauguration of the Book Fair at the Grand Palais, crossing Paris in a tide of two thousand people (always the same ones) who, after having communed in fairground thronging and bookish vanity will meet up again around midnight at the end of a third collective migration, in the small number of Montparnasse restaurants marked with the sign of the tribe. Preceded perhaps by some minister or other, followed as ever by a horde of journalists. You can mark out the trajectory of this *fauna culturalis* every evening in advance, working from the order of the invitations, as in days gone by you could follow popular gatherings from place to place with certainty.

The computer will take over everywhere from the operation of thinking, leaving the brain to lie fallow, as the mechanistic technologies of the nineteenth century have already done with the body. People are becoming increasingly zombie-like. It looks as though their brains have already been removed and they are merely functioning on their spinal chords.

Executives are like joggers. If you stop a jogger, he goes on running on the spot. If you drag an executive away from his business, he goes on running on the spot, pawing the ground, talking business. He never stops hurtling onwards, making decisions and executing them.

The fact that anything should be condemned to disappear feels unbearable to us. But such a feeling is even stronger if it is death which has just disappeared . . .

All the imaginaries of breakup are fading. Children finding it impossible to leave their families. It's the same with couples. They no longer split up. Why bother? Things are just the same everywhere else. You just negotiate your mutual indifference. It's the same with the political situation. Whatever the government, no one's keen to change it, since every alternative illusion is dead. Thus the political relationship has got itself into the same conjugal neurosis as the couple or the rising generation. The price to be paid is that of a low intensity, a scaled-down demand, an air-conditioned intelligence which allows us never to cross the threshold of breakup.

Don't I go on so many journeys merely to avoid moving to another flat? For want of a 'vertical' break, I find a horizontal *modus vivendi*, moving from one horizon to the next without sorting out a very simple situation. All situations develop along the lines of psychoanalysis: they are interminable. Adjustable arrangements, minimal switches, little corrections of trajectory, that is what life is like today. That is the way that, at a deep level, biology and genetics are transforming it into soft psychology and horizontal pragmatics. The end of the vertical dimension, the end of transgressions and prohibitions, the end of revolutions, the end of the orgy.

Indifference to any potentially available solution.

Lunch with Fabius. How naive to seek enlightenment on the art of government from a motley collection of intellectuals and actresses! What do the population want? Why have they no enthusiasm for anything? Why do the efforts made on their behalf produce negative opinion-poll results? It is quite bewildering how this man, who certainly didn't get to be Prime Minister without employing some cunning and who must surely know how much sharp practice, ill will, deceit and pride goes into any successful political career, can be so ingenuous about the perverse mechanisms of popular indifference, deploring the apathy and perfidiousness of the masses, their lack of imagination and participation, the absence of a collective myth, etc. (when it is by virtue of this indifference that he and others like him are in power today), deploring the emptiness of the social world apparently without noticing the void which power itself occupies (which is why he fills that void so wonderfully well). You wonder how he can survive two days in this role and this setting. The people are bored? Then give them something to marvel at. Otherwise they will make their own entertainment at your expense. They will seek out something to astonish them in spectacle (the spectacle of the media or of terrorism) if they cannot find it on the political stage. Individuals and peoples want something to marvel at – that remains their great passion. And nothing you have done has amazed them. Shock them by telling them the truth? Rubbish! Truth is extremely dangerous, since the person who tells it is the first to believe it. Now it only takes a politician believing in what he says for the others to stop believing him: that is the specific perversity of the political field. It's no use just telling the truth; you need the ring of truth too. It's no use lying. You need to have the ring of lying. This is what the socialists will have lacked to the end. They will have lied a lot and told the truth a lot, but they will never have known how to do something that had this ring about it. Now, admittedly, you can pull off quite a political stroke by using the truth – and indeed that was Fabius's intention. But you must never believe in the truth of truth. If you do, you lose all its effect. You have to use truth as a challenge, go beyond what needs to be said for it to be strictly true. The truth must astonish; otherwise, it becomes akin to stupidity. That's what produced all the political tribulations of the Greenpeace Affair. If a prime minister doesn't know that, then he has his head in the clouds. And this is the impression Fabius gives: sure of his ambitions and totally ignorant of the immoral ways of the world. I had before me the Divine Left in person.

Theory does not derive its legitimacy from established facts, but from future events. Its value is not in the past events it can illuminate, but in the shockwave of the events it prefigures. It does not act upon consciousness, but directly on the course of things from which it draws its energy. It therefore has to be distinguished from the academic practice of philosophy and from all that is written with an eye to the history of ideas.

Lusitanian gentilezza. The beauty of Lisbon. Capanica, the cliff of rape. Charnica, fireworks and the popular circus. The palaces beside the Tagus. Linda Lolita. Schubert at the Palácio Queluz. The thieves' market. The restaurant on the beach. The waiter comes back a thousand times to ask if everything is alright, if the wine is cool enough, the fish well grilled, if everyone is happy. When he comes back for the thousand and first time, M. announces clearly, looking him right in the eye, 'Everything is perfect. We are *really happy!'* He is virtually paralysed totally taken aback. He disappears and never returns.

Dunkirk. The excited crowds, the champagne corks popping, the old workers weeping at the launch of the last ship from the dockyard. A mass celebration of the end of work. For nobody actually wants this enormous ship. It is a pure act. It does not even have a name. They did not even dare to baptise it since it is the fruit of the conjoint sterility of Land and Labour, as Marx would say – and I wouldn't mind seeing his face if he could view this bewildering product of the productive forces. It has been given the code number 331. It will merely have served as a pretext for the mania for production, the futile passion for production which still survives today to drive generations to despair. This fabulous object, a testament to the immense useless capacity of man, should immediately be put away in a museum, in a crypt of neon, together with all the workers who are now slaves not of capital, but merely of the legend of work, and who have, in their own lifetimes, become part of the legend of the factories.

Man has lost the basic skill of the ape, the ability to scratch its back. Which gave it extraordinary independence, and the liberty to associate for reasons other than the need for mutual back-scratching.

Trampling down the leaves like snow in the wild light of the dead citadel, whose prince in days gone by rebelled against his king, for which reason the walls were pulled down.

The 'performance' of the Magazini Criminali at Rimini: they transform the slaughter of a horse and its cutting up into a sacrificial ritual for a hundred or so spectators. This stirred up a great flurry. Not unsurprisingly. But what is repugnant in this is not the spectacle of death in itself but that there is no collective sense whatever, either among the actors or among the spectators, among whom all sacrificial values disappeared long ago to be replaced by a worldly semiology of violence and blood.

The equilibrium of the system is always in crisis, but this produces no serious consequences. The needle merely oscillates around a hypothetical centre, a statistical median. The oscillations no longer lead to the system being overturned, since it no longer has a centre of gravity. The 1929 crisis could not recur today. It has been replaced by a perpetual crisis simulation. In the same way, it is possible for the heroic or intrinsic values of a society to collapse, whereas the same values in renovated, simulated, face-lifted form (take Reagan, for example) no longer run the risk of ending in catastrophe. They are no longer in danger of having their weight plunge them to a sticky end. They either float or, like currencies, follow the writhing course of the snake.

We do the same in our own lives: with a float on each side, we go forward oscillating around a hypothetical equilibrium path, keeping our distance from the fatal declinations.

Remembering with emotion the Pompeii of the sixties, still close at that date to the Pompeii of the 1800s, to the one Goethe and the eighteenth-century travellers might have seen, still almost the Pompeii of the excavations and of rural naivety, like an old print. Then going back in one's mind's eye to the beginnings, to the moment of the catastrophe, the absolute dream. Smiling at this incurable nostalgia, these perpetual regrets for what is lost (even the ruins were more beautiful in the past) and yet maintaining the freshness of those regrets.

We read the order or the disorder of the world in the 'major incidents' of world news. The Seveso catastrophe, the Air India Boeing, Beirut Airport, the Heysel tragedy are the only significant events – in contrast to 'political' events – since there is a secret correspondence between them and they thus contain, in a more or less poetic form, all the information in the world. What are we to call them indeed? Dramas, collective psychodramas, accidents, terrorism, plots, catastrophes? They are all these things at once and fascinating for being so indeterminate. They are like the 'black box' of the missing aircraft. Generally it does not tell us much, and in many cases it is not even retrieved. Yet the black box is like a miniature hologram of the whole event. The black boxes converse among themselves; it is up to us to connect in to their wavelength.

In the area around M., absolutely all the crossroads have been replaced by a repulsive form of gyroscopics even more dangerous than the traditional cross-roads. Nothing is finer than two roads crossing. And nothing is more ridiculous than two roads which wind themselves around so as not to touch each other, condemning the road-user to an excessive amount of pointless signalling in the process. The stupidity of currently fashionable technologies: the roads cross without touching – the philosophy of the interchange. Among humans this is called communication.

As soon as he arrives, everyone falls silent. It is like when you're walking in the country and the crickets mysteriously fall quiet. The zone of silence moves with him like an eye, and the shrill noise starts up again as soon as he has passed by. Destiny no longer penetrates into that zone, all is quiet, passions are extinguished, but it is the ideal zone from which to measure the stridency of the world.

The end of every cycle of activity, of suffering or pleasure, is marked by a symbolic masturbation. A sort of mythological offering to seal the end of an event, a nod towards orgasm, the joy of an ending. For societies too, the end of a cycle is marked by a symbolic masturbation, which is followed not long after by real melancholy. This is what socialism was for us.

The famous gesture of tearing one's page from the typewriter, by which writers or journalists elevate themselves to the status of Wild West heroes drawing their six-shooters.

For *America,* only one method: given a certain number of fragments, notes and stories collected over a given time, there *must* be a solution which integrates them *all,* including the most banal, into a necessary whole, without adding or removing any: the very necessity which, beneath the surface, presided over their collection. Making the supposition that this is the only material and the best, because it is secretly ordered by the same thinking, and assuming that everything conceived as part of the same obsession has a meaning and that there must necessarily be a solution to the problem of reconstituting it. The work starts out from the certainty that everything is already there and it will be sufficient simply to find the key.

Information can tell us everything. It has all the answers. But they are answers to questions we have not asked, and which doubtless don't even arise.

In the same way as we need statesmen to spare us the abjection of exercising power, we need scholars to spare us the abjection of knowledge.

Cancer and terrorism both occupy fractal zones. They are born out of the desertified, disintensified, abandoned zones. Today the body and the social are desertified zones.

The driver of the train which crashed killing forty-two admits that he did indeed see the signal, that he even recorded it in the black box, but that he did not slow down. Reflex registration, but not followed by action. Automatic reaction to the sign, but not to the content. Closed circuit of brain and machine. Interaction with the black box, but not with the world. This is the deep logic of communications – being connected in to the sign and making a sign in return, responding to signs with signs rather than with acts. It is therefore the very logic of communication which produces accidents of this type, and not some human or organizational failing.

Cancer: the code breaks down, becomes disorganized, lets cells proliferate indiscriminately. A disease of information.

AIDS: the immune system (the secret defences of the body) is suppressed. Obsessive fear of contiguity, of flows (sperm, blood, saliva), of contact. A disease of communication.

What if all this reflected a brute, instinctive refusal of the flows of communication, of sperm, of sex, of words? If there were in all this an 'instinctive', vital resistance to the extension of flows and circuits – at the cost of a new mortal pathology, AIDS and cancer, which would ultimately be protecting us from something even more serious, or would at least be serving as an alarm signal? After all, neurosis is what man invents to protect him from madness.

Supposing it had been possible to predict the Mexico City earthquake to within an hour, what would have been the most urgent task? To evacuate the population or to organize getting the pictures to the world's media? In the sub-conscious of every journalist, the idea lingers that one has, on this occasion, lost the best pictures of the catastrophe. If the earthquake had been predicted, who would have missed the satellite pictures? Nobody. In Italy too, in 1981, the media got there before the emergency services.

One might even wonder whether, had it been possible to arrange a rendez-vous before the catastrophe, a crowd of sightseers wouldn't have converged on Mexico City. Whole charters of eager snobs would have arrived, to replace the Mexicans who would have run away.

Exalting the chorus, whipping up the cirrus, shaking off the virus, extolling the tonus, glorifying the habitus, mystifying the stratus, balancing the abscissus, terrifying the impetus.

We are entering a period of intense cadaverousness and our imaginations are simply not up to it. Here too we must choose and make our own personal obituaries. Is this a foretaste of the end of the century?

Everything today – the launching of a newspaper, a ship, a commercially ruinous aircraft, a road network, a new missile or a cultural programme – is justified in the last instance by the fact that it creates jobs. This argument, which is itself devoid of meaning, is our alibi, our last rites, our Extreme Unction.

Beyond a certain threshold of expenditure, energy reaches a stage of super-cooling. Once lovemaking has been repeated often enough, it can go on indefinitely. The hysteresis is total, energy expenditure reaches a high, the principle of economy is suspended. The five-man bicycle in Jarry's *Supermale* even used the energy of a dead man. The corpse kept on pedalling. He even pedalled better than he had when he was alive, since he no longer had any problems. It is the death drive which multiplies motor or erotic effects, by the inertia principle.

In an airliner, before landing: 'Ladies and Gentlemen, your Unconscious please!'*

Falling in love, for the space of an evening, with the harpist in the Paris Opera orchestra, with her low cut black dress and gold necklace. The fluttering of her eyelids and lashes, the movements of her hands and eyes, held my attention better than Berio's pretentious scenography. The musicians were, in any case, more attractive than the actors and their little pleasures, their secretive nods and winks, their dumb show in the orchestra pit all had much more truth about it than the ridiculous drama being played out above their heads.

Nothing can match the loneliness of a pianist in a large hotel. All around him is just a hum of cocktails and small talk; he is more alone with his melody than he would be on an island. Yet, at a particular moment, he stops and people applaud. You are doubly astonished: there was an end to this music then, and people were listening? He was playing something and he was not playing in vain? He seems stupefied himself. But he well knows, in the secret depths of his soul, that this applause only breaks out because his music has fallen silent, a silence these wild

*A play on the similar sounds, especially when spoken over a tannoy, of *'votre attention'* and *'votre inconscient'*. [Tr.]

222

things notice in much the same way they notice the sugar melting in their glasses. So, like the bald prima donna, he quickly starts up with a new tune.

The scapegoat is not what he once was. No longer is he hounded; now he is pitied (the rights of man, dissidents, the *'beurs'*,* etc.). But he is the scapegoat nonetheless and it is still the same.

When there is a solution, it is no longer a real problem.
When there is an answer, it is no longer a real question.
For at that point, the problem is part of the solution and the answer is part of the question.
And then nothing remains but solutions without problems and answers without questions.
O, happy days when we had only questions without answers and problems without solutions!

Human rights, dissidence, antiracism, SOS-this, SOS-that: these are soft, easy, *post coitum historicum* ideologies, 'after-the-orgy' ideologies for an easy-going generation which has known neither hard ideologies nor radical philosophies. The ideology of a generation which is neo-sentimental in its politics too, which has rediscovered altruism, conviviality, international charity and the individual bleeding heart. Emotional outpourings, solidarity, cosmopolitan emotiveness, multi-media pathos: all soft values harshly condemned by the Nietzschean, Marxo-Freudian age (but also the age of Rimbaud, Jarry and the Situationists). A

*Second-generation French citizens of North African origin. [Tr.]

new generation, that of the spoilt children of the crisis, whereas the preceding one was that of the accursed children of history.

These romantic, worldly young people, imperious and sentimental, are re-finding the poetic prose of the heart and, at the same time, the path of business. For they are the contemporaries of the new entrepreneurs and they are themselves wonderful media animals. Transcendental, P.R. idealism. With an eye for money, changing fashions, high-powered careers – all things scorned by the hard generations. A soft immorality, a low-grade sensuality. A soft ambition too: that of a generation which has already been successful in everything, which has everything going for it, which practises solidarity with ease, which no longer bears the stigmata of the curse of class. They are the European Yuppies.

Print-out of existence
Existential design
Death on a turnkey basis
Not the infinite: the exponential

As the end of the century approaches, all our culture is like the culture of flies at the beginning of winter. Having lost their agility, dreamy and demented, they turn slowly about the window in the first icy mists of morning. They give themselves a last wash and brush-up, their ocellated eyes roll, and they fall down the curtains.

In front of the lens, the temptation is to stand still, as a defensive reflex. But it is the same on the other side of the lens, when you take a photo: you stand still and empty yourself of your substance for a brief moment to take the object by surprise.

The softening of thought began with open-heart ideology: the New Philosophers. It continued with the New Romantics. Then the revival of philosophy in
general. Then the euphoria of new enterprise and new business. The social
'naturalism' of neoliberalism. Everywhere face-lifted values have reinstalled
themselves, a touching dynamism, a puerile religiosity, in which love resurfaces
blithely. A way for the horde to close ranks at the time of the greatest dispersion
of the species.

Zinoviev doesn't give a damn about the Western intelligentsia, with its
subtlety and sophistication. He knows that the massive unintelligible reality on the
other side of the iron curtain is more interesting than our dialectical, interactive
processes. He draws the power of his irony from the power of stupidity. The gist
of what he is saying is that if we have not conquered this stupidity, you are not
going to overcome it. And he is only too damned right. Or he is saying this: you
are behind us in absolute terms, because we have been through the worst, whereas
you still have it to go through. You cannot argue with that. Dissidents? In the case
of Sakharov, says Zinoviev, the Western world and the Eastern bloc *derive equal
benefit* from this lamentable situation and are equally responsible for it. You have
no hope of converting us for we are a more advanced form, the post-catastrophe
social form, the form of survival. You are still in the realm of life, but we are
already in the realm of afterlife – survival. In any case, your society is artificial: it
goes to any lengths to sustain illusions from which we have already drawn all the
possible consequences. Do not hope for communism to evolve, for it is you who
quite peaceably will take the same path as we have. You are already a lot like us.

Does the West want the Soviet bloc to dissolve, to liberalize, to break up? Not
at all, for it would lose what serves it as ideology in the process: the existence of
the opposing bloc to which it is structurally bound. The liquefaction of that glacial

block would affect the whole defence system and profile of Western values for the worse, simply by disseminating them into infinity. Exactly as the melting of the ice-caps would change for the worse the level of the oceans, wiping out the inhabited continents, expunging their frontiers from our memories. If the entire Soviet bloc melted in the heat of human rights, it would represent a catastrophe for the West which would be equivalent to the sudden melting of the polar ice-caps, or even to the catastrophe which, in its day, the unleashing of the tidal wave of Soviet gold-reserves on the world market would have represented. What good would it be then to speak of the socialist hell? It has exactly those infernal qualities necessary to sustain the fiction of our paradisiacal universe. If it is not in itself just, it is completely justified by this role it plays in the structure of a world equilibrium and the survival of our own values. These values themselves have no absolute value in relation to any human purpose whatever (no objective divinity certifies the human superiority of the Western over the Eastern bloc), they only have a merely relative value in this well-ordered opposition between heaven and hell.

We are to some extent the equivalent of the nineteenth-century '*sublimes*': elective situation, distinctive character, virtue, the daemon of philosophy, the daemon of critical craftwork, a regal indifference to industrial development.

When the question of human rights has been swept away, we shall see emerge a relative preference for the absence of freedom, both in the East and in the West, in the South and the North. We shall then be down to the real problem. Zinoviev is the paradoxical thinker of this state of affairs. Of servitude linked with the realization of models, of a lack of distinction between heaven and hell.

Christo's art finds an erotic and aesthetic quality in dressing things, whereas we have long been used to the vulgarity of an aesthetics of undressing. Bad advertising glorifies things by making them visible, all too visible. Christo ennobles a form by covering it up. He produces a kind of enigmatic advertising for it, and this is directly in line with a distinction made by Baudelaire: the true artists are those who give the commodity a heroic status, whereas the bourgeois are only capable of giving it, in advertising, a sentimental status.

To wrap up the ground – to clothe it – is to give back to the town, to the street, the charm of an inner space, of a maternal public space like the one you find in some Italian towns. Particularly when the hot, veiled sun of September is in harmony with the general effect of a veiled calligraphy.

Simulacra are today accepted everywhere in their realist version: simulacra exist, simulation exists. It is the intellectual and fashionable version of this vulgarization which is the worst: all is sign, signs have abolished reality, etc. Who would have thought ten years ago that the sign would so quickly have become part of this kind of stereotyped language? Like 'proletariat', 'dialectics' and 'the unconscious'. These terms won't even have made it to the year 2000.

The Tempest acted by mongols before an ultra-chic audience of ministers and stars. Kennedy Foundation. All the Shakespearian mongols will be received tomorrow by the Pope. A society's flirtation with its worst dregs. Who are the mongols right now?

The rich never give you anything (dixit A.). Wealth is unrelenting; it always screws you. Those who are rich in intelligence, power and beauty don't give much away either. They make you pay all the more for the fact that their capital is symbolic.

Comparing that unrelenting face of wealth with Countess Bathory who tortured young peasant girls. She at least was tortured herself, walled up in total darkness, in absolute silence and her own excrement, with a hole in the wall for food to be passed through. The bloodbaths she had taken gave her the savage energy to hold out for two years in the dark.

Thinking of those happy days while walking around in the backstreets of Rome. Here everything is deeply incestuous, though in a different way from Elisabeth Bathory for whom all those peasant girls were her daughters whose incest was to be sealed with blood. But that was a sadistic and violent incest, whereas the whole Roman culture practises a gentle, spiritual incest. Akin to fetishism: that of the mamma, the sister, the young adolescent, the Virgin and the Saints, all swirling about in the same incestuous spiral. The carnal perfection of the detail, the carnal softness of the marble, the lewd transparency of the fountains – little navels of the squares set deep in the backstreets – and the water which streams down from them. The miracle of a faultless urbanity, a total civility – even the ruins share in this. However far back you go in Italy, there has never been any nature. There has only ever been a baroque figuration.

The Ideal Woman is like the Città Ideale. A pure, deserted form, with a few blinds raised to reveal a cool and meaningless shade, with a few houseplants poking out, and sometimes an allegorical item of linen.

There have already been situations in which the sexes seemed to be distancing themselves from one another once and for all, by sublimation or chastity, or, as today, by oscillation of differences. At the end of the Roman Empire and the end of the Middle Ages. An end-of-the-world atmosphere – a millenarian atmosphere – either frantically throws the sexes together or irremediably moves them apart.

Seducing for a woman consists in sliding into an empty place, where her ideal form is already traced out by all those of her sex who have preceded her. For a woman, seducing is the act of an animal species, and all women are accomplices in the tiniest such venture undertaken by one of their number. There is a chain of feminine seduction. For his part, a man is faced with a mammoth task: braving, with each woman, the image and the collusive judgement of all the others. The game is an unequal one, and it is easy to see why he is less and less willing to risk it. In any case, woman has always kept the captivating part of seduction for herself (the temptress), whereas he has always ended up with the faintly ridiculous part (the seducer). Now it is difficult for a man to join in a game of being a sex object, and in a way simulate femininity. For there is no chain of masculine seduction. It is impossible for him to collude with other men in being a desirable object, as women do among themselves. There is no secret pact to protect a man in such an undertaking.

The day the world ends, no one will be there, just as no one was there when it began. This is a scandal. Such a scandal for the human race that it is indeed capable collectively, out of spite, of hastening the end of the world by all possible means just so it can enjoy the show.

Little tribal ceremony among intellectuals on Fifth Avenue to discuss the end of the world. It might seem a terrific idea to talk about this in New York of all places since this is the world's epicentre, but, on reflection, there is no sense in the idea, since New York already is the end of the world. There is no sense reflecting on this in miniature in a scenario which is necessarily inferior to its model. Except the very requirement that we should rescue the *idea* of the end of the world from its real occurrence – which is the habitual labour of intellectuals.

Challenger and Chernobyl: the only felicitous accidents, like a freeze-frame of the system. In the same way as a photo arrests movement and restores the unforgettable character that it had lost, the Challenger explosion has revived our imagination where space is concerned. The photos of Challenger were only so beautiful because they fixed in our minds the secret destination of the adventure of space travel, whereas its speed only gives us the apparent movement.

From the holocaust to the hologram: a fine programme.

You can only take good photographs in brilliant light, on perfectly clear days, or under a leaden grey sky. The colours stand out in both cases, either by their brilliance or their mutedness. Similarly, you only write well in states of total illumination or of deep melancholy.

I arrive, by a snow-covered path, at a kind of château. The room I enter by is covered all over with several inches of snow – even on the furniture and the ceiling. Shining in through the window are fierce, fluorescent advertisements in blue and red. I walk through the huge rooms secretively. I once lived here. Voices come near. I feel worried, since these are important men and I have no right to be here. But their voices change, their eyes change too, and suddenly they become mental defectives. The mansion is an asylum and indeed a nurse is stretched out on a long table in the peristyle. I wake up, retaining an exact impression of having once been mad myself in this very place, in a previous life.

Laugh of the female
Spectre of the death-rattle laugh of the female
Intermittent laugh of an albino female onlooker
Transparent sex of a female onlooker
End of the world on Fifth Avenue
itch for collapse
collapse of the itch
Ontological fistulas   Hare-brained notions
Impure lips   expure lips
Ethics of agony.

It might be objected that we are going to be able to watch the origin of the world thanks to the prodigious telescopes which enable us to trace back, from nebulae to quasars, the course of the original Big Bang. The traces of the origin are still there in space; we simply have to go back through them. But the problem is that they are moving further and further away into the future. We shall never reach this horizon where the fragments of universes contemporaneous with the beginnings of the world are to be seen. Thus the origin will never take place for us. And there will consequently be no end either, since the only end lies in re-establishing contact with the origin.

Today, a Monday, having written all the articles, replied to all my mail (at last!), obtained my doctorate and finished off *America*; for the first time for perhaps ten or twenty years, I realize I have nothing else to do. No projects, no constraints. Everything that was pending has been finished, and whatever else comes from this point on will, in a sense, be part of a supplementary existence, separated from the other one by this moment of lightness, of emptiness, of astonishment and relief – a unique moment no doubt, which demands to be saluted as it passes. I observed a minute's silence in its honour.

The Cynecure. Looking for the Cynecure (in the palinody of my cenesthesias, as Segalen would say). The Sabbatical form.

What was the Stoic dream of our adolescence – detachment – suddenly materializes in maturity. I now find myself out on my own, within a rainbow-hued research structure.

Towns are never left alone; there are always works going on – digging, demolition, construction. Knocking down, building up again. Perhaps only certain places in California, completely anaesthetized by domestic luxury and suburban comfort, seem to have come to rest in a fixed and lasting ambience, beyond this perpetual deconstruction. Works are always going on in our bodies too. They are constantly being disturbed, tortured, renovated. Never at rest, never serene. Peace of mind – impossible to keep it more than a few hours. Impatience always gets the upper hand. Everyone aspires to peace and quiet, but they do so today in a thoroughly derisory manner, wherein we see the last moments of the contemplative soul. In the countryside there is always a dog howling. And sterility is hereditary.

There are things one can no longer talk about or cannot yet talk about again. Their ghosts have not yet been stabilized. Marxism?

There are others we cannot talk about yet, or can no longer talk about, because their ghosts are already running around the streets; they are already preceded by their shades. Information, communication?

One only speaks well of what is disappearing. The class struggle, the dialectic in Marx, power and sexuality in Foucault. Analysis itself contributes to hastening their end.

Sliding like a reptile along the mental moquette
zero mentality
Crawling like the paralytic dog
towards the agitated sea
Like the last squatters of the catacombs of the political
politically suave
metaphysically svelte
Dialogues of the Dead   Jubilees   Extreme Unction
Pure obituary of the end of the century
Luxurious Serenity
Spectrum Reality
*Inconditional Shit**

California is not what it was
Rome too is not what it was
No more imperial cities
No more crazy societies
Where is one to go?
Berlin   Vancouver   Samarkand?

*Last three lines in English in original. [Tr.]

This journal is a subtle matrix of idleness.